USDA

United States
Department of
Agriculture

Forest
Service

Northern
Research Station

General Technical
Report NRS-116

ForGATE - A Forest Sector Greenhouse Gas Assessment Tool for Maine: Calibration and Overview

Chris Hennigar
Luke Amos-Binks
Ryan Cameron

John Gunn
David A. MacLean
Mark Twery

Abstract

This report describes the background calibration, inputs, and outputs of ForGATE, a forest sector greenhouse gas (GHG) accounting tool designed primarily to communicate information relevant to the evaluation of projected net GHG exchange in the context of Maine's forests, the Northeast forest sector, and alternative national or regional carbon (C) accounting guidelines. It also provides forest managers and policy makers with an easy-to-use tool for examining the relative merit (C credit revenue vs. project cost) of C offset projects and forest sector life cycle GHG accounting. GHG accounts include: 1) storage in aboveground and belowground live biomass and dead organic matter components; 2) storage in forest products in use and in landfill; 3) forest sector emissions by harvest, transport, and mills, or avoided emissions (substitution, bioenergy); as well as 4) landfill methane release and avoided emissions from methane energy capture. Different forest and forest product pools can be included in result summaries to reflect different C accounting guidelines (e.g., Climate Action Reserve, Voluntary Carbon Standard). Results can be compared for baseline and C offset project scenarios. Where possible, the marginal differences between baseline and project scenario performance indicators are calculated. All forest-level emission or storage measures are expressed in tonnes of CO_2 equivalents for comparison purposes. Finally, economic indicators such as net present value and benefit-cost ratios for C offset projects can be evaluated using alternative assumptions for the value of stumpage, C credits, and offset project costs. The user enters their own inventory of stand type area by treatment regime data for baseline and offset project scenarios and can quickly adjust many GHG accounting parameters. ForGATE is available without charge from http://www.nrs.fs.fed.us/tools/forgate/.

Authors

CHRIS HENNINGAR is a research associate with the Faculty of Forestry and Environmental Management, University of New Brunswick, P.O. Box 4400, Fredericton, New Brunswick, E3B 5A3, CANADA. To contact, call 506-447-3339 or email at chris.hennigar@unb.ca.

LUKE AMOS-BINKS is a research assistant with the Faculty of Forestry and Environmental Management at the University of New Brunswick.

RYAN CAMERON is a research associate with the Faculty of Forestry and Environmental Management at the University of New Brunswick.

JOHN GUNN was the senior program leader at the Manomet Center for Conservation Sciences in Brunswick, ME, and is currently the executive director of the Spatial Informatics Group-Natural Assets Laboratory in Hebron, ME.

DAVID A. MacLEAN is a professor with the Faculty of Forestry and Environmental Management at the University of New Brunswick.

MARK TWERY is a research forester with the U.S. Forest Service, Northern Research Station in Burlington, VT.

Cover Photo

Hemlock trail; photo by Mark Twery, U.S. Forest Service

Manuscript received for publication April 2012

Published by: For additional copies:

USDA FOREST SERVICE   USDA Forest Service
11 CAMPUS BLVD., SUITE 200   Publications Distribution
NEWTOWN SQUARE, PA 19073-3294   359 Main Road
                                                              Delaware, OH 43015-8640
May 2013   Fax: 740-368-0152

Visit our homepage at: **http://www.nrs.fs.fed.us/**

CONTENTS

INTRODUCTION

Forests play a major role in removing CO_2, the primary greenhouse gas (GHG), from the atmosphere through carbon (C) sequestration. Forests in the United States sequester 10 percent of the country's CO_2 emissions each year (Woodbury et al. 2007). Globally, conversion of forest to nonforest accounts for about 12-15 percent of all CO_2 emissions (van der Werf et al. 2009). Carbon markets and regional climate change policies are developing that allow emitters of GHG to offset their emissions through C sequestration projects. However, the role of actively-managed forests remains unclear, in part because we do not know how they can best be used to sequester C when a full life cycle assessment of forest products is not considered (Lippke et al. 2011). It is not always clear when it would be better to grow trees for longer periods of time to a larger size (more C on the stump) versus having short rotations that sequester C in forest products, allowing yet more sequestration in the woods. Without a full life cycle assessment of C sequestered by managed forests, policy makers may create mitigation policies that are actually counterproductive to influencing climate change over the long-term.

The estimated value of the global forest C market was $178 million in 2010 and could play an important role in both helping to retain forests and maintain the forest products industry (Diaz et al. 2011). However, with complex forest offset protocols and relatively low per tonne prices, few foresters are willing to invest the time and money to calculate GHG profiles for their land bases and operations, let alone explore alternate management strategies to reduce GHG emissions. The complexities and costs of stand growth modeling, forest and forest product C accounting, and emissions tracking across forest sector activities pose a significant barrier to most resource professionals. There are many mitigation opportunities to explore including reducing harvest to store more C in the forest, increasing biomass harvest of tree tops and branches for biofuel to displace use of coal, or installing an additional biomass boiler at a mill to reduce fossil fuel energy consumption. Many of the key drivers for C emissions of the forest sector are beyond the forest manager and reside in the policy realm. Here we present a tool for landowners and policymakers to evaluate the GHG implications of different forest management options and assumptions such as mill electricity and fuel sources, landfill methane capture, and percentage of pulpwood used as biofuel.

Elements of a life cycle assessment approach were used to develop ForGATE, a forest sector GHG assessment tool in Microsoft Excel® spreadsheet software (version 2010)[1]. This tool enables foresters and GHG offset project analysts to quickly explore and rank the merits of alternative silvicultural strategies, product use (e.g., bioenergy vs. lumber) scenarios, and methods of waste disposal (burn or landfill) on net GHG exchange (emissions minus sequestration). ForGATE provides the means to explore sensitivity of results to different mill energy sources, efficiency of wood and methane conversion to electricity, methane capture rates at landfills, and assumptions about product substitution and external leakage. Leakage occurs when a supply from one source is reduced and causes a corresponding increase in supply from other sources due to a consistent demand for a particular resource. Users can enter forest acreage by broad stand type (90 combinations of species group, size class, and crown closure) and silvicultural regime to characterize their current forest inventory and baseline management plan, and compare this to alternative scenarios. The net GHG balance and difference between strategies across a range of C pools and emission sources over time is concisely summarized for the user to evaluate emissions impacts over 100 and 300 year time horizons.

---

[1] The use of trade or firm names in this publication is for reader information and does not imply endorsement by the U.S. Department of Agriculture of any product or service.

ForGATE TOOL

ForGATE was primarily designed to broadly communicate relevant GHG life cycle accounting information for Maine's forests, the Northeastern forest sector, and alternative national or regional carbon (C) accounting guidelines. It also provides forest managers and policy makers with an easy-to-use tool for examining the relative merit (C credit revenue vs. project cost) of C offset projects and forest sector life cycle GHG accounting.

Forest C accounting within ForGATE relies upon precompiled simulation summaries of Maine Forest Inventory and Analysis (FIA) permanent sample plots measured from 2002 through 2006 projected forward with the the Forest Vegetation Simulator Northeast Variant (FVS-NE, version 08/10/11) (Crookston and Dixon 2005, Dixon and Keyser 2008). FVS-NE was used to simulate stand growth, calculate tree pulpwood and sawtimber volumes, and estimate C contained in live and dead forest organic matter over time. Following harvest, forest product C dynamics and associated GHG emissions from forest sector activities were accounted for using the Carbon Object Tracker (Hennigar et al. 2008) model and summarized temporally by broad forest type and treatment classes for representation in ForGATE. See later sections for details on model calibration and summary calculations for ForGATE.

GHG accounts in ForGATE include: 1) storage in above- and belowground live biomass and dead organic matter components; 2) storage in forest products currently in use and in landfills; 3) forest sector emissions by harvest, transport, and mill type, and avoided emissions as a result of substitution or bioenergy; as well as 4) landfill methane release and avoided emissions from methane energy capture. Summary results using different C accounting guidelines (e.g., Climate Action Reserve, Voluntary Carbon Standard) can be presented by modifying the individual forest and forest product pools reported in the results worksheets.

Because many stand and forest-level assumptions were simplified to make ForGATE manageable in Microsoft Excel®, ForGATE should not be used for marketable forest C accounting projects where accuracy and need for specific landowner forest inventory, management plans, and forest successional transitions following disturbance may be required. However, ForGATE can be used to quickly compare relative differences in net GHG exchange between multiple project scenarios under broad forest types and treatments and user-defined assumptions about energy sources, wood use, and landfill management.

It provides an efficient preliminary analysis of the relative merit of a large number of potential forest management or forest product use offset projects from which a subset can be selected for more accurate examination by integrating accounting methods and information disseminated here into the client's preferred forest-estate modeling framework.

Background Assumptions and Calibration

To use ForGATE, the user is only required to enter current acreage by stand type and an allocation of the current acreage to the seven predefined silviculture regimes. It is assumed in ForGATE that each acre allocated to a given stand type and regime continues to be managed under the same regime. Forest succession and regrowth following disturbance are fixed as inherent outcomes of the underlying Forest Vegetation Simulator Northeast Variant (FVS-NE) and regeneration assumptions used here. Because ForGATE excludes complex treatment scheduling and successional transition pathways, stand-level annual outputs of key performance indicators (e.g., harvest, live and dead C storage, mill greenhouse gas emissions, energy use) across simulations can be readily calculated. The primary purpose of ForGATE is to summarize stand-level key performance indicators at the forest level for user-defined area by stand type and management regimes. ForGATE uses a table of 21 key performance indicators by stand type and silvicultural regime precompiled from over 50,000 FVS-NE simulations in concert with background calculations of forest and forest product C storage and ensuing CO_2 equivalent (CO_2e) emissions or energy consumption from harvest and downstream activities. Carbon dioxide equivalency is a quantity that describes, for a given mixture and amount of greenhouse gas, the amount of CO_2 that would have the same time-integrated radiative forcing (global warming potential [GWP]), when measured over a specified timescale (generally, 100 years). A generalized list of these key indicators is given in Table 1. Calculation logic and conceptual basis for use in ForGATE is described below.

Under regimented management conditions and because no catastrophic natural disturbances (e.g., spruce budworm, fire, wind storms, climate change) were modeled, we can reasonably infer that over a time period of 100-300 years, the forest will move toward either: 1) an old-growth, late-successional condition if no harvest occurs; or 2) a regulated distribution of stand development stages (young to mature) that would allow for sustained annual harvest. If current live biomass and dead organic matter C inventory conditions for all stand types are known (starting conditions; initialized with forest inventory data) and we can estimate the future upper bound storage potential of stand types at the forest level under alternate management regimes (ending conditions; mean storage from 100-300 years predicted by FVS-NE), then we can make forest-level approximations about long-term temporal rates of C loss or sequestration under

Table 1.—List of stand-level measures used for background calculations by ForGATE with respective units and simulation time period(s) used to quantify the measure

Stand-level indicator	Units	Measurement period (years)
Current 2010 inventory of forest live and dead biomass pools [a]	t C/ac	2010
Projected maximum potential steady state pool inventory [b c]		
Forest live and dead biomass [a]	t C/ac	Mean 2150-2310
Wood in use [b]	t C/ac	Mean 2210-2310
Paper in use [b]	t C/ac	Mean 2040-2310
Degradable landfill [b]	t C/ac	Mean 2210-2310
Methane from landfill in atmosphere (100-yr GWP basis) [b]	t CO_2e/ac/yr	Mean 2210-2310
Projected rate of pool growth [d]		
Merchantable volume harvested [b]	ft³/ac/yr	2010-2310
Energy potential of pulpwood harvested	kWh/ac/yr	2010-2310
Energy potential of tops and branches harvested	kWh/ac/yr	2010-2310
Structural wood products [b]	t C/ac/yr	2010-2310
Primary and secondary transport emissions [b]	t CO_2e/ac/yr	2010-2310
Mill energy (fossil fuels) required for steam [b]	t CO_2e/ac/yr	2010-2310
Mill grid electricity required [b]	GJ/ac/yr	2010-2310
Saw mill energy requirements for steam [b]	kWh/ac/yr	2010-2310
Wood waste [b]	t C/ac/yr	2010-2310
Paper waste (net of recycling) [b]	t C/ac/yr	2010-2310
Landfill methane release [b]	t CO_2e/ac/yr	2010-2310

[a] Applies to the following pools in ForGATE: i) aboveground biomass, ii) belowground biomass, iii) standing-dead, iv) down-dead, v) forest floor, and vi) belowground dead organic matter.

[b] In ForGATE, these measures are further broken down by forest product to finished-product pathways: i) pulpwood: paper, ii) pulpwood: finished wood product, iii) sawlog: paper product, and iv) sawlog: finished wood product.

[c] Measured as a function of pool inventory levels averaged between the onset year of steady state conditions (≥90% of levels at 300 years) and 300 years (end of simulation). Forest and paper storage approached steady-state conditions after 150 years and 40 years of management, respectively.

[d] Measured as inventory accumulation by 2310 divided by total simulation years (300).

different forest inventory conditions and management regimes. Given these assumptions about long-term C dynamics, we also assume that: 1) no impacts from natural disturbance or climate change will occur; 2) there is a sustained harvest at the forest level from a regulated age-class distribution of managed stands throughout the simulation; and 3) the forest-level upper-bound C storage potential of a given forest pool for a designated stand type and management regime is sufficiently characterized by the mean C storage levels predicted between 150-300 years for all stand type by management simulations. These assumptions underlie the majority of forest-level calculations in ForGATE for pools that are shown to eventually reach a steady state condition. These include mostly biologically-based pools where absolute pool decay would eventually match pool sequestration (forest biomass), or inputs from production (wood and paper in use, degradable landfill storage, and landfill methane persisting in the atmosphere). These pools fluctuate from one harvest rotation to the next for individual stands; however, at the forest level, assuming a regulated or old-growth forest age structure condition, all pools approached steady state before 300 years.

The maximum inventory potential of each pool can therefore be characterized as a function of pool inventory levels averaged between the onset year of near steady state conditions (defined here as ≥ 90 percent of level at 300 years) and 300 years (end of simulation). For paper in use, when expressed at the forest level, steady state conditions were apparent after only 30 years (Table 1). In comparison, all other forest product pools did not approach steady state conditions until 200 years (Table 1). Other forest-level pool dynamics were better characterized by estimating a fixed rate of pool accumulation over time. Examples of such pools include emissions from harvest, transport, and mills, consumption of forest-derived products (pulpwood, tree tops and limbs, finished structural wood products), or pools having extremely slow decomposition rates (non-degradable C stored in landfills).

Where possible, downstream stand-level outputs (e.g., mill activity, pulp used for energy) are expressed in terms of total or average energy required (steam production) or energy potentials (pulpwood) rather than CO_2e produced or avoided (Table 1). As discussed in the GHG emissions section, this was done to avoid fixing values for a large number of assumptions regarding regional energy sources (coal, natural gas, hydro), landfill management (methane capture systems or use, percentage of wood waste going to landfill or energy), and amount of avoided emissions from using wood over other, more fossil fuel-intensive alternatives. By doing so, ForGATE passes control of these assumptions back to the user through four worksheets that can be calibrated to reflect local harvest productivity, regional grid electricity and other energy sources, landfill management, amount of emissions avoided per unit of wood used for energy, and more. These assumptions can be varied by baseline and C offset project scenarios within ForGATE so that sensitivity of these assumptions with respect to net GHG balances can be easily evaluated. Default national and regional values are provided from the literature for all user-defined assumption parameters. Depending on availability of regional values, some parameters may not be specific to Maine. Detailed assumptions and information sources used in ForGATE are provided in Appendix A.

Description of Worksheets

ForGATE includes 12 worksheets. including 3 sheets that provide background information, 2 sheets that define forest area by stand type and management regimes (baseline forest vs. C offset project forest management), 4 sheets containing forest sector GHG modeling assumptions that can be modified by the user (harvest, mill, landfill, avoided emissions), and 3 worksheets that present forest-level results over 300 years for a number of key GHG, harvest, and economic performance indicators, respectively. These results are presented for baseline and C offset project scenarios. Where possible, the marginal differences between baseline and project scenario performance indicators are calculated. All greenhouse gas emission and C stock change measures are expressed in carbon dioxide equivalents.

Step-by-step instructions are provided on the first introductory worksheet and in the section below to familiarize the user with successive ForGATE worksheets and required inputs. The worksheets within the Excel model contain further descriptions of spreadsheet contents as well as extensive cell comments to describe specific values, assumption, and references used. ForGATE is available without charge and can be downloaded from the USDA Forest Service, Northern Research Station web site (http://www.nrs.fs.fed.us/tools/forgate/).

Each number below corresponds directly to the order and number of worksheets in ForGATE:

Introductory worksheets

0) **Preface:** Describes steps to use ForGATE.
1) **Forest:** Briefly describes forest information and modeling.
2) **Silviculture:** Briefly describes harvest regimes (rotation length, % removals, and stand eligibility).
3) **Forest Products:** Briefly describes forest product C accounting.

Forest management input worksheets

4) **Forest Baseline:** Defines the baseline forest management scenario. User inputs current acreage by stand type and then allocates the amount of each type that is being managed under the seven predefined silviculture regimes.
5) **Forest Offset Project:** Defines the offset project forest management scenario. Input the same current acreage by stand type and amount as input for **Forest Baseline**. Allocation of acreage across silvicultural regimes can vary from the baseline.

Emission assumption dashboards

6) **Mill:** Used to alter mill energy input source(s) assumptions (e.g., coal, natural gas, wind, or use a mean of many different sources). Assumptions can differ between baseline and offset project scenarios. Useful for understanding the sensitivity of the offset project to local conditions. Further described in the manufacturing energy and emissions factors section of this paper.

7) **Landfill:** Used to alter assumptions about wood waste management at landfill such as percent degradable wood and paper used for energy and methane capture rates. See the forest and forest product carbon accounting section for more information.

8) **Avoided Emissions:** Used to change avoided emission potential assumptions (Table 2) with respect to using wood (methane, biofuel, solid wood products) over other more fossil fuel intensive alternatives (see the avoided emission section). Assumptions that can be altered:

   a. Global warming indices (t CO_2e/kWh) for landfill methane and biofuel as well as alternative energy sources (coal, wind, etc.);

   b. Percent of available pulpwood or tree tops and limbs harvested that can be used for energy production;

   c. Percent of wood products produced that substitute for (displace) the use of other more fossil fuel intensive alternatives (e.g., steel and concrete) and by how much per mass of C stored in the finished wood product.

Results: key performance indicators for baseline and offset project scenarios

9) **Harvest Outputs:** Area managed and volume harvested per acre per year by treatment.

10) **GHG Emissions:** Net GHG emissions (sequestration – emissions) broken down by forest, forest product, and forest sector after 10, 20, 50, 100, 150, 200, and 300 years (see GHG emissions results worksheet section).

11) **Economics:** Marginal differences between baseline and offset project net revenue as a function of stumpage, discount rates, C-credit value, and trading costs (See section on Economics results worksheet and Table 3).

Step-By-Step Worksheet Guide

Step 1: Understand forest landscape classification (stand type attribute definitions) used in this calculator; see worksheet **Forest**.

Step 2: Understand the seven silviculture regimes (operability constraints, % removals and residual targets post-harvest) that were modeled in FVS for each forest type in this calculator by reviewing information in worksheet **Silviculture**.

Table 2.—Pools tracked (accounted) at the forest level by ForGATE, and usage in various contemporary GHG reporting standards in the United States

Category	ForGATE pools (accounts)	GHG reporting standard [a]				
		1605(b)	CAR	VCS	CCX	RGGI
Forest	Aboveground live biomass	X	X	X	X	X
	Belowground live biomass	X	X	X [b]	X	X
	Standing dead wood	X	X	X [b]		X [b]
	Down dead wood	X	X	X [b]		X [b]
	Forest floor dead	X	X [b]	X [b]		
	Belowground dead	X	X [b]	X [b]		
Forest product	Paper in use	X	X [b]	X [b]	X [b]	X [b]
	Wood in use	X	X [b]	X [b]	X [b]	X [b]
	Landfill storage	X	X [b]	X [b]	X [b]	X [b]
	Landfill CH4 emissions					
Operation emissions	Harvest					
	Wood transport to mills and between mills					
	Timber mills					
	Paper mills					
Avoided emissions	Landfill CH$_4$ energy capture					
	Landfill wood waste energy capture					
	Tree tops and limb biomass used as biofuel					
	Pulpwood biomass used as biofuel					
	Wood product substitution[c]					

[a] Information adapted from Galik et al. (2009b; Table 1); 1605(b) = U.S. Environmental Protection Agency, CAR = Climate Action Registry, VCS = Voluntary Carbon Standard, CCX = Chicago Climate Exchange, RGGI = Regional Green House Gas Initiative.

[b] Optional.

[c] Avoided emissions from using wood products over more fossil fuel intensive substitutes such as steel or concrete in residential and commercial structures.

Step 3: Enter your acreage by forest type and amount allocated to seven alternative silviculture regimes or reserve (no management) based on your current (baseline) management plan in worksheet **Forest Baseline**.

Note: because FVS tree lists were derived from the Maine FIA database, only stand type (species group, crown closure class, size class) combinations that existed in the current inventory are available (90 out of 96 possible combinations). If your forest contains stand type definitions that are not available in this Worksheet, then you must append those acres to a similar stand type that is defined.

Step 4: Same as step 3; however, here you can alter the acres allocated to each silviculture regime in worksheet **Forest Offset Project** to explore the influence of management on GHG emissions in worksheet **GHG Emissions**.

Note: total acreage by forest type must remain unchanged.

Step 5: Understand models and literature used to calibrate off-site forest product carbon retention dynamics in-use (e.g., in homes) and disposed in landfills in worksheet: **Forest Products**.

Step 6: Alter mill energy input source(s) (e.g., coal, natural gas, wind, or use a mean of many different sources) for your region in worksheet **Mill Emissions**. Assumptions can differ between baseline and off-set project scenarios.

Step 7: Alter wood waste management at landfill assumptions such as percent degradable wood and paper, methane capture rates, and percent wood waste used for energy for your region in worksheet **Landfill**. Assumptions can differ between baseline and off-set project scenarios.

Step 8: Alter displaced or avoided emission assumptions in worksheet **Avoided Emissions**: 1) global warming indices (t CO_2e/kWh) for use of methane and wood energy feedstock and mean baseline alternative energy source (coal, wind, etc.) global warming index; 2) percent of available pulpwood or tree tops and limbs harvested that can be used for energy production; 3) percent of wood products produced that substitute (displace) the use of other more fossil fuel intensive (e.g., steel and concrete) and by how much per tonne of C stored in the finished wood product.

Step 9: View forest-level live biomass inventory, off-site C retention in forest products, and downstream (mill and landfill emissions) GHG emissions (t CO_2e) for Baseline and Off-set Project after 10, 20, 50, 100, 150, 200, and 300 years in worksheet **GHG Emissions**. Difference in total effective GHG emissions (emissions – storage change) between scenarios is shown as well as other forest-level statistics. Comparisons of forest management and economic metrics are presented in worksheets **Harvest Outputs** and **Economics**. The **Harvest Outputs** worksheet outlines differences in harvest outcomes dictated by the different management strategies employed by the baseline and forest carbon offset projects. The **Economics** worksheet shows differences in economic outcomes and indicators for the baseline scenario and the forest offset project. Some inputs are required to quantify costs associated with the carbon offset project and will effect results.

Greenhouse Gas (GHG) Emissions Results Worksheet

The GHG Emissions worksheet in ForGATE quantifies net emission differences between baseline and offset project scenarios. The worksheet calculates CO_2e inventory change or emissions across a number of pools (Table 2). Users can choose which pools to include in the GHG Emissions results summaries. ForGATE tracks pools that are currently accounted for under a variety of contemporary reporting guidelines identified in Table 2 (based on Galik et al. 2009b). Additional ForGATE pools not accounted for within any known forest management reporting guidelines (e.g., mill emissions, landfill methane emissions, avoided emissions from product substitution) are included to allow users to more holistically explore cross-sector benefits or impacts of forest management on global net GHG emissions. These measures can be useful for policy-level decisionmaking and sensitivity analyses.

ForGATE was not designed to estimate initial inventory levels of forest product C storage or sector emissions from historically derived forest sector activities. Therefore, all pool inventory levels other than forest biomass are assumed to start at zero in ForGATE. For all pools that are expected to approach a steady state eventually, forest inventory levels were linearly interpolated between starting levels (2010) and maximum potential levels at the onset year of steady state conditions (Table 1) and then remained constant until 2310. These calculations are apparent within the cells of the GHG Emissions worksheet. For all other pools projected to accrue indefinitely (e.g., harvest emissions), inventory levels were estimated from the annual fixed rate of pool accrual (described in the GHG section) by stand type and stand management multiplied by the simulation year and by the amount of area stated by the user in each stand type and stand management condition.

Depending on the reporting standard, the accounting definition of the baseline can change (e.g., base year, modified base year, single-practice performance standard; see Table 1 in Galik et al. 2009b for more details). The baseline scenario in ForGATE is estimated as a function of projected C emissions minus C sequestered over time that best approximates what would have been done in the absence of the offset project. It is up to the user to enter assumptions about current or proposed area allocated to each stand type and silviculture regime (see **Forest Baseline** worksheet).

Most reporting guidelines will reduce an offset project's eligible forest C credits by some fixed and proportional amount to account for: 1) project leakage (Murray et al. 2004), and 2) project reversals from potential errors in inventory or modeling and threat of natural disturbances over the project lifetime. Depending on the reporting standard, these adjustments can devalue additional forest C storage from 0-43 percent (Galik et al. 2009b). Assumptions regarding leakage, start-up project costs, and natural disturbance insurance can be specified under the Economics worksheet and are only applicable to economic result summaries presented in that worksheet.

Economics Results Worksheet

Potential economic benefits are important indicators when considering the viability of a C offset project and are presented in the Economics worksheet of ForGATE. Revenues attained from a C offset project are largely dependent on market price of C credits, which can fluctuate like any commodity. Prices for contracts traded on the Chicago Climate Exchange ranged from $0.73 on May 7, 2004, to $7.40 on May 30, 2008 (Bilek et al. 2009). Considerable costs can be incurred in the start-up stage of a C offset project in order to register and properly fulfill contractual obligations. Recurring costs occur at regular intervals in order to finance the maintenance of a project including verification and monitoring. Revenues from the sale of harvested wood products are determined based on stumpage rates ($/ft^3) and annual volume production of harvested wood products. Stumpage rates represent the value of wood products after all extraction costs have been deducted. Table 3 outlines the inputs used to parameterize the Economics worksheet of ForGATE.

Only those C credits that are produced in excess of the baseline scenario are eligible to be traded. As a result, the gross number of credits produced by the baseline scenario is subtracted from those produced by the C offset project to determine the net gain in C credits over and above the status quo. Due to the extended time period for which the landowner must commit to the proposed C offset project, a certain percentage of the accumulated C credits, known as the C reserve buffer (Table 3), must be deducted to account for unforeseen natural disturbances that would reduce C storage projected during the commitment period. A further deduction from the net gain in C credits is made in order to account for leakage in the C system. The resulting number of credits following these deductions is then eligible to be sold on the market.

Those C credits that are eligible to be sold on a C credit exchange produce revenue but are subject to market fluctuations. For example, the average price for offsets across the primary forest carbon markets rose from $3.8/tCO$_2$e in 2008 to $4.5/tCO$_2$e in 2009 and up to $5.5/tCO$_2$e in 2010 (Diaz et al. 2011). Costs fall into two categories that are input into the **Economics** worksheet (Table 3) of ForGATE: 1) Project establishment costs including start-up investments, project development, baseline calculations, and initial verification fees; and 2) recurring project costs such as modeling, verification reports, and inventory costs. Default

Table 3.—Inputs required to parameterize the economic section of the carbon (C) offset project calculator

Measure	Unit	Description
Revenues		
C credits in	$/t CO$_2$e	Market value of C credits attained by C offset project
Hardwood pulpwood	$/ft^3	Stumpage revenue from hardwood pulpwood
Hardwood timber	$/ft^3	Stumpage revenue from hardwood timber
Softwood pulp	$/ft^3	Stumpage revenue from softwood pulpwood
Softwood timber	$/ft^3	Stumpage revenue from softwood timber
Project establishment costs		
Start-up investments	$	Investment costs for project establishment (e.g., equipment).
Project development	$/ac	Fees associated with scoping, planning, and project documentation
Baseline calculations	$/ac	Determination of baseline carbon from inventory
Initial verification fees	$/ac	Verification fees required to establish and register project
Recurring project costs		
Modeling	$/ac	Modeling required for monitoring of offset project at regular intervals
Verification report	$/ac	Verification report due at regular intervals
Inventory costs	$/ac	Recurring inventory costs required for reverification
Other variables		
Verification interval	yr	Number of years between reassessment of C offset project
Trading fee	$/t CO$_2$e	Fee charged as a commission on sales of C credits on a carbon exchange
Reserve buffer	%	Percent of C credits held in reserve to buffer against unforeseen disturbances
Aggregation fee	%	Fee charged in order to aggregate C credits from multiple landowners to facilitate sale on a C exchange
Leakage	%	Reduction in carbon credits due to leakage. Occurs when a reduction in supply from one source results in an increase in supply from another source due to market demands.
Plantation cost	$/ac	Cost of planting one acre of land
Annual discount rate	%	Annual discount rate used in the calculation of net present value.

ForGATE values were taken from Galik et al. (2009a). Net revenue is determined by adding net revenues from harvested wood products (stumpage – planting costs) to net revenue obtained from selling C credits (market value – project costs).

In order to facilitate comparisons of economic outcomes between the baseline scenario and the C offset project cumulative net revenue, net present value and a benefit/cost ratio are calculated and presented in the **Economics** worksheet of ForGATE. Cumulative net revenue is a running tally of all revenues subtracted by costs and is broken down by the contribution to the C offset project from timber harvest and C credits. The internal rate of return is the expected rate of return for an investment based on a series of corresponding cash flows and is presented at 10, 20, 50, and 100 years from the beginning of the offset project. Net present value is useful to appraise the long-term suitability of projects because it measures the time value of money as an investment occurs during the initial phase of the C offset project. A user-defined discount rate in the **Economics** worksheet is used to discount future cash flows and initial start-up costs to help assess the viability of the project. Net present value is shown for the baseline scenario and the C offset project (Fig. 1). In order to assess how well the C offset project performs economically against the baseline scenario, a benefit/cost ratio was determined. Benefit was defined as the net present value of C credits produced by the C offset project divided by the difference between the net present value of harvest operations for the baseline project and the C offset project. A benefit cost ratio of 1 would indicate that the C offset project was able to attain the same net present value as the baseline scenario.

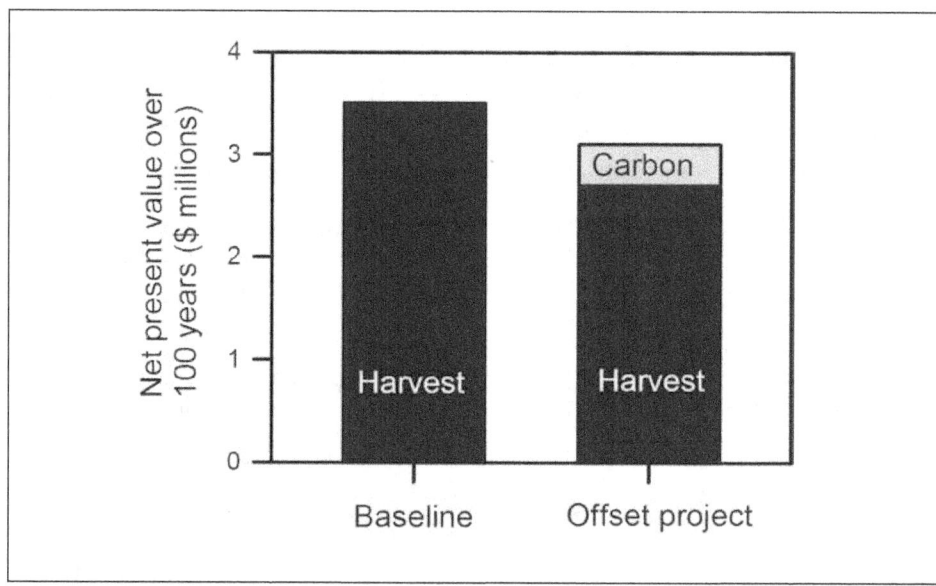

Figure 1.—Net present value (NPV) of the baseline scenario and the offset project by net revenue source (stumpage from timber harvest or carbon traded for offset project).

FOREST INVENTORY AND STAND GROWTH MODELING

Forest C stock accounting within ForGATE relies upon the forest management modeling results of baseline statewide forest data. We used Maine Forest Inventory and Analysis permanent sample plots measured from 2002 through 2006 to characterize the state's current forest conditions. A total of 6,278 subplots (four subplots per FIA plot) were considered as separate inventory samples because stand conditions and structure often vary widely between subplots within plots.

The Forest Vegetation Simulator Northeast Variant was used to simulate stand growth and to calculate tree pulpwood and sawtimber volumes. FVS-NE is a distance-independent, individual tree-based stand growth model used by forest practitioners and scientists to forecast stand growth and yield. This model simulates complex forest management activities and estimates C contained in live and dead forest organic matter and in forest products, both currently in use and in landfills. These carbon values are accepted by voluntary C markets (e.g., Climate Action Reserve 2010) to estimate C stock changes in managed forests.

For this project it was important to use FVS-NE for C accounting transparency and because it allowed modeling of management effects on C stocks. However, it should be noted that practitioners in the Acadian Forest region (Quebec, Nova Scotia, New Brunswick, Maine) generally agree that FVS-NE does not always produce realistic forecasts of forest growth for the Acadian forest (Ray et al. 2008, Saunders et al. 2008). Currently, the only widely-supported model for Maine is FVS-NE; however, the calibration of a new FVS Acadian forest variant for this region is underway.

The IPCC (2003) recommends an accounting period sufficient to categorize net GHG emission trends over at least 3-4 harvest rotations, which would equate to 200-300 years in the northeast United States. Each FIA subplot was projected from the measurement year (2002-2006) to 2010 to quantify initial inventory conditions and was then projected for an additional 300 years to quantify long-term forest biomass stock changes and harvest outputs (timber and pulp volume/ area/yr). Projections were determined by hardwood and softwood components and for the seven silvicultural regimes and the no silviculture regime.

FVS-NE Calibration

Estimates of current and long-term forest C stocks by stand type are key components for calibrating ForGATE. For all simulations, tree growth was first calibrated with the FVS-NE internal growth-calibration process using periodic FIA tree-level growth increments for the previous measurement period. Sensitivity analyses using Jenkins et al. (2003) were performed to test whether long-term FVS-NE projections of stand structure (quadratic mean diameter and number of stems) remained within the range of current forest inventory conditions.

Overall, there were substantial differences between long-term predictions from the base FVS-NE model (no additional calibration) and the range of forest conditions reported in the current inventory. For the base FVS-NE model, basal area reached an unrealistic 390-435 ft^2/ac (90-100 m^2/ha) in some stand projections in as little as 50-100 years. Also, most trees, regardless of species, persisted in the stand for hundreds of years. These unrealistically dense stands with very large old trees led to an over prediction of long-term forest aboveground biomass. Projections estimated that within 100 years, aboveground biomass would triple that of the current mean aboveground biomass measured in Maine FIA permanent sample plots (PSP). Over 300 years, aboveground forest biomass on average was projected to quadruple current levels and be nearly 25-75 oven-dry t/ac above maximum inventoried levels (95th percentile).

The FVS-NE does not directly adjust mortality by tree age or size. Mortality is largely driven by background mortality rates and stand density. Therefore, low to moderately stocked stands had very low levels of projected mortality regardless of tree age or size. In an attempt to resolve this problem, our calibration to the base FVS-NE model introduced species-specific tree mortality when tree diameter at breast height (d.b.h.) was greater than or equal to the lesser of: 1) maximum d.b.h. recorded in the FIA dataset (2001-2006) by species, or 2) the upper bound d.b.h. estimated within two standard deviations of the mean tree d.b.h. in the FIA dataset (2001-2006). Mortality of large trees was set at 10 percent in each simulation period to avoid rapid stand breakup. Example d.b.h. constraints are shown in Table 4 for common commercial tree species. In addition, spruce-fir (*Picea* spp. A. Dietr. and *Abies balsamea* [L.] Mill.) stands were projected to accrue significantly more basal area than the current inventory 95th percentile (47 m^2/ha). Therefore, the maximum basal area limit for spruce-fir dominated stand types was reduced from about 55 to 50 m^2/ha, as recommended by Saunders et al. (2008).

Table 4.—Maximum d.b.h. and two standard deviations from the mean d.b.h. recorded by species measured in north-eastern Canada and Maine (Weiskittel et al. 2010; p. 46) and the Maine FIA permanent sample plot (PSP) dataset (2001-2006)

| | | d.b.h. (inches) | | | |
| | | North-eastern Canada and Maine | | Maine FIA-PSP | |
Common species name	Scientific species name	Max	95th percentile	Max	95th percentile
Balsam fir	*Abies balsamea* (L.) Mill.	37	9	19	10
Black spruce	*Picea mariana* (Mill.) B.S.P.	39	9	18	11
Red spruce	*Picea rubens* Sarg.	47	12	37	14
Red maple	*Acer rubrum* L.	32	12	25	14
Paper birch	*Betula papyrifera* Marshall	28	11	21	12
Sugar maple	*Acer saccharum* Marshall	42	14	34	17
White spruce	*Picea glauca* (Moench) Voss	27	13	27	15
White cedar	*Thuja occidentalis* L.	39	13	30	15
Yellow birch	*Betula alleghaniensis* Britton	39	15	39	17
Eastern hemlock	*Tsuga canadensis* (L.) Carrière	35	16	28	16
American beech	*Fagus grandifolia* Ehrh.	26	13	22	14
White pine	*Pinus strobus* L.	44	19	35	20
Quaking aspen	*Populus tremuloides* Michx.	27	13	22	15

Regionally calibrated regeneration inputs during FVS simulations are necessary to increase model accuracy in projections greater than 20 years (Bankowski et al. 1996). FVS-NE contains a partial establishment model capable of simulating stump sprouting following harvest and allows for manual insertion of new stem ingrowth by species, height, d.b.h., percent survival, and age using FVS command-line keywords (Dixon 2002). Tree sprouting was simulated to occur following any harvest of those species that can sprout. FVS keyword commands were developed to dynamically model the frequency and species composition of ingrowth of 2 inch d.b.h. trees in each model growth cycle as a function of stand basal area, percent hardwood basal area, tree count, geo-climactic site productivity (Weiskittel et al. 2011), and species composition according to Li et al. (2011). Ingrowth trees were assumed to be 10 years old and 10 ft in height. The ingrowth model developed by Li et al. (2011) was fit for a wide geographic range of low to overstocked forest conditions measured from permanent sample plots throughout Maine and southeastern Canada and will be incorporated into the new FVS Acadian Varian currently under development.[1]

---

[1] Weiskittel, A. July 2011. Personal communication. Assistant Professor of Forest Biometrics and Modeling, School of Forest Resources, University of Maine, 229 Nutting Hall, Orono, ME 04469-5793.

Although the ingrowth model used here was fit for a wide range of forest conditions, regeneration abundance following moderate to heavy harvest may be underestimated for stands with low numbers of trees (<500) and low basal area (<50 ft^2/ac) because these stand conditions were outside the range of data used to fit the ingrowth model. For these specific stand conditions, regeneration was instead modeled as a function of pre-harvest species composition and shade tolerance. We compiled average species composition for each forest type (Table 5) (Arner et al. 2001) present in Maine's FIA subplots. To account for the effect of increased forest floor light on regeneration composition following harvest, species composition proportions for each forest type were adjusted to favor shade-intolerant species over shade-tolerant species by adjusting proportions up (factor of 1.75) and down (factor of 0.25), respectively. Species of intermediate tolerance such as white pine (*Pinus strobus* L.) were not adjusted. Additional FVS command keywords were used to introduce a regeneration pulse (1800 new stems, 2 years old, and 2 feet in height) of these species proportioned dynamically by forest type following heavy harvest. While it is likely that greater than1800 small stems would be established on sites following heavy harvest in Maine (Brissette 1996, Schofield 2003), introduction of less than or equal to 1800 stems per growth cycle is recommended to avoid prediction bias resulting from extreme tree densities modeled in FVS (Ray et al. 2008).

Introducing both tree size limits and ingrowth greatly improved long-term model predictions of stand structure. With these adjustments, stand conditions (quadratic mean diameter and stem count ratios) forecasted over 300 years remained within the range of conditions in the existing inventory. The modifications described above were applied for all FVS simulations used to calibrate ForGATE.

Stand Type Classification

To make analysis within ForGATE more manageable, a broad forest landscape classification of 96 possible stand type combinations including eight species groups (Table 5), four crown closure classes (Table 6), and three stand structural size classes (Table 7) was developed using a regional expert panel approach. Because projections were derived from Maine FIA subplots, only stand type (species group, crown closure class, size class) combinations that exist in the current inventory are available, resulting in 90 out of 96 possible combinations. Stand structural and compositional statistics for each subplot in 2010 were reported using the FVS strata class summary (FVS_StrClass) and stand summary (FVS_Summary_East) database reports. For forest stand types that are not available in ForGATE, the user should consider grouping those acres with a similar stand type that is defined.

Table 5.—Eight stand species groups used in ForGATE simplified from forest types used by FVS-NE

| ForGATE species group | FVS-NE forest type [a] | |
	ID	Description
Eastern Cedar	127	Northern white-cedar
Eastern Hemlock	105	Eastern hemlock
Intolerant Hardwood	515	Chestnut oak/black oak/scarlet oak
	519	Red maple/oak
	608	Sweetbay/swamp tupelo/red maple
	701	Black ash/American elm/red maple
	705	Sycamore/pecan/American elm
	706	Sugarberry/hackberry/elm/green ash
	707	Silver maple/American elm
	708	Red maple/lowland
	802	Black cherry
	803	Cherry/ash/yellow-poplar
	809	Red maple/upland
	901	Aspen
	902	Paper birch
	904	Balsam poplar
Mixedwood	401	Eastern white pine/northern red oak/white ash
	409	Other pine/hardwood
Other Softwood	102	Red pine
	126	Tamarack
	167	Pitch pine
	383	Other exotic softwoods
Spruce-Fir	121	Balsam fir
	122	White spruce
	123	Red spruce
	124	Red spruce/balsam fir
	125	Black spruce
Tolerant (Northern) Hardwood	503	White oak/red oak/hickory
	504	White oak
	505	Northern red oak
	801	Sugar maple/beech/yellow birch
	805	Hard maple/basswood
White Pine	103	Eastern white pine
	104	Eastern white pine/eastern hemlock

[a] Only forest types present in the forest inventory data were included. Forest type for each inventory sample was assigned using FVS-NE and the FVS_Summary_East database report.

Table 6.—Crown closure classification represented in ForGATE

Crown Closure Class	Total canopy cover (%) [a]
A	85-100
B	67-84
C	33-66
D	<33

[a] Based on Total % Cover reported by the FVS_StrataClass report; calculated for each inventory sample using FVS-NE.

Table 7.—Structural tree-level and stand-level rules used by FVS to classify stand size class (Appendix B in Dixon 2002). FVS stand size classes were used in ForGATE.

Tree size class [a]	d.b.h. class boundaries	
	Softwoods	Hardwoods
Seedling-sapling	d.b.h.<5"	d.b.h.<5"
Pole timber	5"<d.b.h.<9"	5"<d.b.h.<11"
Sawtimber	d.b.h.>9"	d.b.h.>11"

Stand size class [b]	Code [c]	Condition
Sawtimber	1	Pole timber stocking<Sawtimber stocking
Pole timber	2	Pole timber stocking>Sawtimber stocking
Seedling-sapling	3	Seedling-sapling stocking>50% of total stocking

[a] Tree size class is based on tree diameter at breast height (d.b.h.).
[b] Stand size class is based on stand composition of tree size classes.
[c] Available from FVS in the "FVS_Summary_East" report.

Silvicultural Prescriptions

Eight different silvicultural regimes (Table 8) were modeled in simulations for each subplot using a combination of FVS conditional harvest entry rules. Regimes cover a wide range of rotation intervals, operability limits, and target percent removals, and correspond to common or possible treatments (including no management) in Maine forests.

For all harvest entries, total merchantable (pulp and timber) volume had to be $\geq$ 2500 ft^3/ac to ensure economically viable operations, except for second entry shelterwood overstory removal. Minimum rotation lengths (30-100 years) (Table 8), percent basal area removal, and retention targets were based on consultation with foresters. Default FVS-NE species harvest preferences (ranks) were used, and a minimum stem d.b.h. harvest constraint of 5 inches was set for all treatments. Tree selection criteria for individual selection method harvest entries were used to promote a diameter distribution q-ratio of 1.4. The q-ratio is the ratio of the number of trees in a diameter class to the number of trees in the next larger class (Nyland 1998). Selection method harvest was also constrained by 1) a target residual basal area of $\geq$50 ft^2/ac; 2) a maximum d.b.h. cut class of 24 inches; and 3) a 30-yr return interval. Complex FVS keywords used to implement these selection treatment rules were derived from individual tree selection method management choices and dialogs available in the Suppose application (Crookston 1997) downloadable with FVS at http://www.fs.fed.us/fmsc/fvs/variants/ne.php.

Table 8.—Silviculture regimes represented in ForGATE, developed to cover a range of probable or potential treatment options in Maine

Silviculture regime	Rotation target (years)	Stand conditions required for entry [a]	Basal area removal (%)	Residual basal area target (ft²) [a]
No silviculture	-	-	-	-
Clearcut 60	≥60	≥2500 ft³	100	-
Clearcut 100	≥100	≥2500 ft³	100	-
Clearcut-thin				
i) plant 1000 black spruce	≥70 years	-	100	-
ii) thin from below	≥40 post plant	≥1000 ft³	≤40	>40
iii) clearcut	≥30 post thin	≥2500 ft³	100	-
Partial harvest (thin from above)	≥30	>100 ft² and >2500 ft³	≤30	>70
Heavy harvest (thin from above)	≥50	≥2500 ft³	≥60	>40
Shelterwood				
i) 1st entry thin from below	≥70	>2500 ft³	≤60	>60
ii) 2nd entry thin from above	10 years post 1st entry	-	100 overstory	-
Selection method-				
Thin from below without species preference	>30	>2500 ft³	30	>70

[a] Area and volume measurements are expressed per acre. Area always refers to basal area, and volume always refers to merchantable pulp and timber volume.

FOREST AND FOREST PRODUCT CARBON ACCOUNTING

Live and Dead Forest Carbon Storage

Aboveground live biomass (foliage, branches, stemwood, bark, stump) and belowground live biomass (coarse roots) were calculated at the tree level from FVS tree list projection reports using allometric biomass equations (Jenkins et al. 2003) and adjusted using volume-biomass expansion factors following methods from Heath et al. (2009) and Woudenberg et al. (2010). Using biomass correction factors resulted in a 20-40 percent reduction in aboveground live biomass estimates, depending on stand composition and structure, compared to using Jenkins et al. (2003) without correction factors. Tree-level biomass measures were summarized by hardwood (HW) and softwood (SW) species for each FVS projection iteration. Examples of tree-level live biomass calculations, equations, and parameters are available at http://ncasi.uml.edu/COLE/XLS/.

FVS-NE was used to project standing and downed deadwood C and forest floor and belowground dead organic matter C for each inventory sample across all treatments over 300 years. Carbon reporting methods and assumptions for these dead pools are provided in detail within the FVS Fire and Fuels Extension Addendum document (Reinhardt et al. 2009).

Tracking Carbon in Wood Through Harvest, Manufacturing, and End Uses

Minimum d.b.h. and top diameter limits for pulpwood and sawtimber were based on default FVS settings (Dixon and Keyser 2008). Tree-level pulpwood to sawtimber ratios were calculated from net merchantable pulpwood and sawtimber volumes output from FVS tree list projection reports. These ratios were applied to merchantable stem biomass to calculate pulpwood and sawtimber biomass per tree. Pulpwood and sawtimber biomass was summarized at the stand level for each subplot and simulation year by commercial SW and HW groups. Biomass was multiplied by 0.5 to yield C (IPCC 2003). One hundred percent of merchantable roundwood from harvested trees was assumed to be removed from the harvest site. Recovery efficiency of harvest residues (tree tops above 4 inch diameter and branches excluding foliage) from individual trees was assumed to be 43 percent for SW and 67 percent for HW (Cormier and Ryans 2006, Carle 2011). These estimates are generally within the range of percent removals reported from SW and HW harvested sites in Maine (Briedis et al. 2011).

The Carbon Object Tracker (CO$_T$) model (Hennigar et al. 2008) was used to track C removed from forest SW and HW pulpwood, sawtimber, and harvest residues and transferred to C pools in harvested roundwood, finished wood products, wood products in use, landfills, and decomposition (Fig. 2). Harvest residues and roundwood bark were considered to be immediately transferred to the

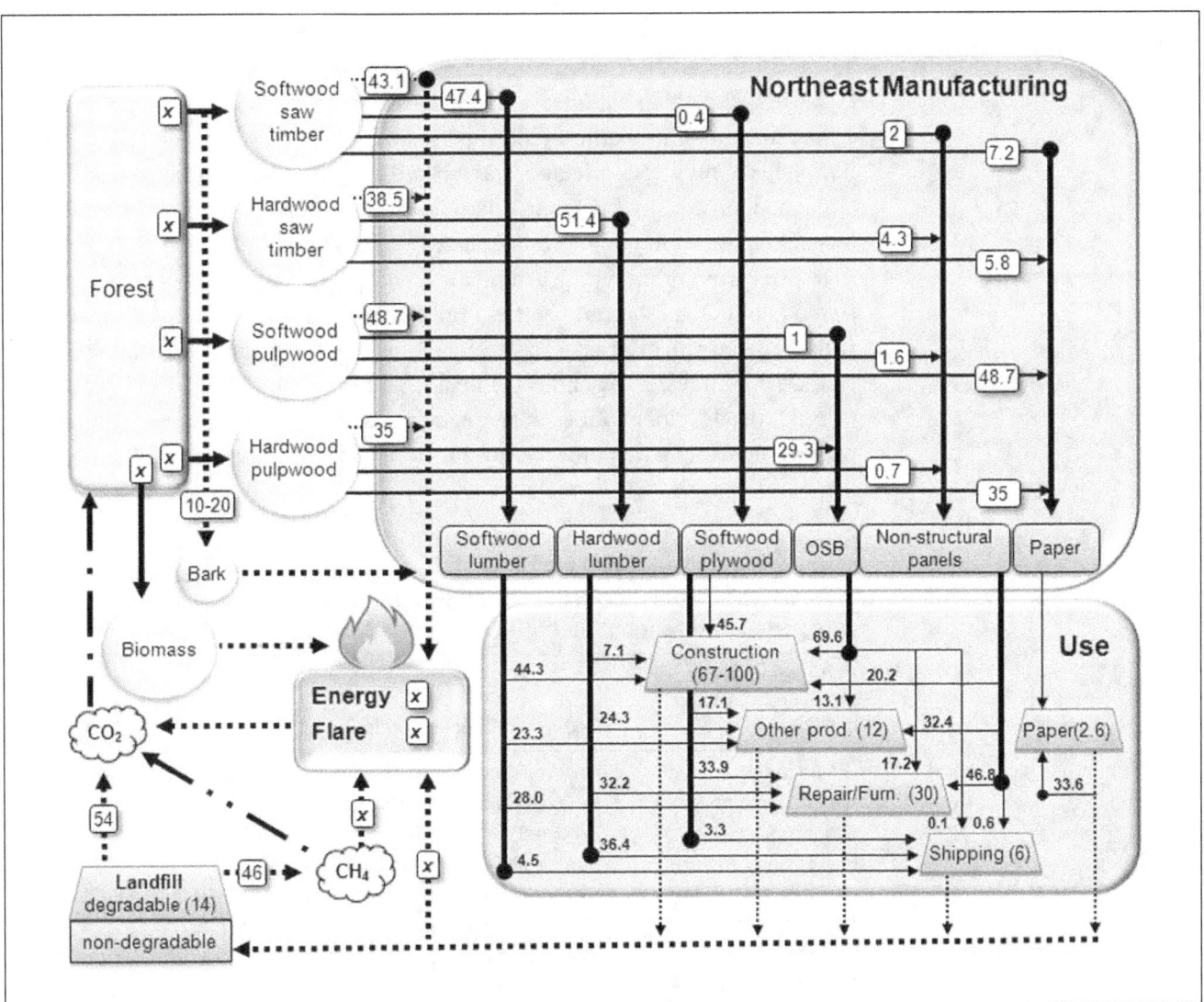

Figure 2.—Carbon transfer (%) from forest to product pools and release to the atmosphere via manufacturing, use, and waste disposal; adapted from forest product carbon reporting standards for the northeast United States (Smith et al. 2006). Carbon in harvest products (circles) delivered to manufacturing facilities is transferred to end-use wood products or the atmosphere (combusted for heat, steam production, or waste disposal). Decay rate of carbon in end-use product and degradable landfill pools (trapezoids) depend on pool half-life (Table 9; Fig. 3); note "Construction" pool contains three subpools: single- and multi-family homes and commercial buildings, each with different half-lives (Table 9) and material input proportions (Table 10), which were omitted from this figure for simplicity. Landfill degradable CH$_4$ emissions are based on NCASI (2004). Transfer boxes shown as x indicate that the quantity transferred varied depending on stand type or treatment (e.g., forest pool), or was varied to test sensitivity on results (e.g., % CH$_4$ capture; see text for details). Line format (solid, dotted) is only used to clarify pathways.

atmosphere in the year of harvest. In all cases, to avoid double counting C stock losses from forest and wood products, we assumed C released from combusted wood did not result in CO_2 emissions. This is done because C losses from the forest are tracked explicitly and any C release from immediate combustion of harvested material will be inherently accounted by the reduction in C storage in the forest C pool. This capability negates the need to assume C neutrality of C released from wood used for biofuel. Mill roundwood utilization statistics, product end use, and landfill decay rates defined by Smith et al. (2006) were adapted for parameterization of CO_T. Smith et al. (2006) estimated roundwood C transfer, excluding bark, from SW and HW pulpwood and sawtimber through: 1) manufacturing into primary finished products including SW and HW lumber, SW and HW plywood, oriented strand board (OSB), nonstructural panels (e.g., medium density fiberboard, particleboard), and pulp/paper and waste by geographic region in the United States (Table D6 in Smith et al. 2006); and 2) transfer from primary finished products into 16 end-use products ranging from single family homes to railroad ties (Table D2 in Smith et al. 2006). Products with the same rate of decay (Table 9) were aggregated to simplify primary to end-use pool transfer dynamics in the model (Table 10). A fixed decay yield (Fig. 3) was developed for each aggregated product group for representation within CO_T using a first order decay equation and respective product half-lives listed in Table 9.

Table 9.—Aggregated C retention pools simulated by the Carbon Object Tracker (CO_T; Hennigar et al. 2008) and relationship to end use product categories and respective half-lives defined by Smith et al. (2006; Table D3)

End-use product pool groups represented in CO_T	End-use product categories	Half-life (years)
Single family homes	New residential construction: single family	100
Multi-family homes	New residential construction: multifamily	70
Other products	New residential construction: mobile homes	12
Repair and furniture	Residential upkeep and improvement	30
Commercial buildings	New nonresidential construction: all except railroads	67
Other products	New nonresidential construction: railroad ties	12
Other products	New nonresidential construction: railcar repair	12
Repair and furniture	Manufacturing: household furniture	30
Repair and furniture	Manufacturing: commercial furniture	30
Other products	Manufacturing: other products	12
Shipping	Shipping: wooden containers	6
Shipping	Shipping: pallets	6
Shipping	Shipping: dunnage, etc.	6
Other products	Other uses for lumber and panels	12
Other products	Solid wood exports	12
Paper	Paper	2.6

Note: Single and multi-family homes and commercial buildings are listed as "Construction" in Figure 2 for brevity but are tracked separately in CO_T.

Table 10.—Percentage of primary wood products transferred annually to end-use product groups (Table 9) in the United States (adapted from Smith et al. 2006)

Primary wood product [a]	Construction (homes and commercial)			Other products	Repair and furniture	Shipping
	Single family	Multi-family	Commercial buildings			
Softwood lumber [b]	33.2	3.1	7.9	23.3	28.0	4.5
Hardwood lumber [b]	3.9	0.4	2.8	24.3	32.2	36.4
Softwood plywood	33.4	3.3	9.0	17.1	33.9	3.3
Oriented strand-board	57.8	4.7	7.1	13.1	17.2	0.1
Nonstructural panels [c]	13.0	1.9	5.3	32.4	46.8	0.6

[a] Adapted from Table D2 in Smith et al. (2006).
[b] Includes other industrial products as defined in Smith et al. (2006; Table D6).
[c] Includes hardwood plywood as defined in Smith et al. (2006; Table D6).

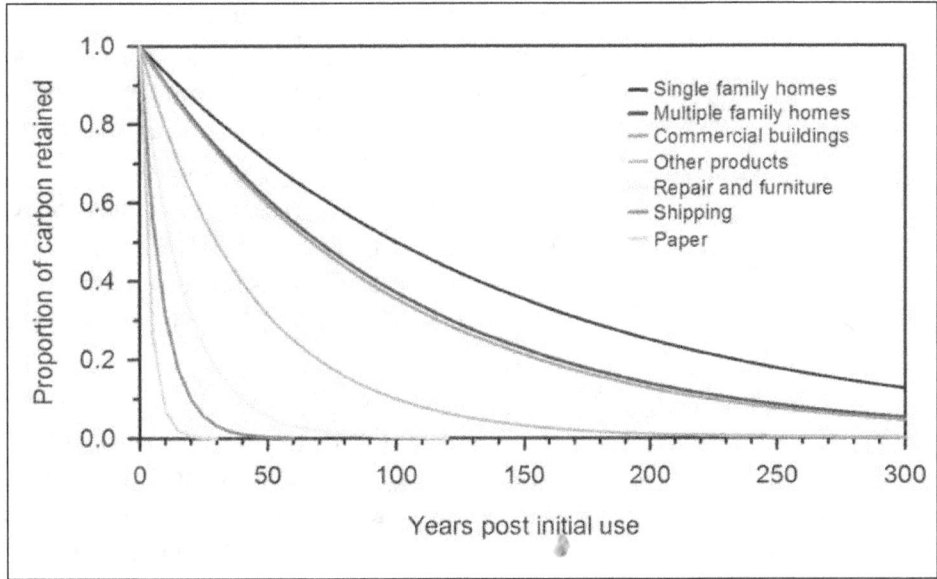

Figure 3.—Proportion of carbon remaining for seven end-use products over 300 years, where year 0 corresponds to year of manufacture. Values calculated using decay equations from Smith et al. (2006).

Disposal and Methane Emission Assumptions

Carbon lost during mill processing or released from end-use products over time is assumed to be transferred immediately to the atmosphere (combusted). In the case of paper, 33.6 percent is recycled or deposited in landfills (Fig. 2). Wood and paper landfill deposition proportions have consistently declined 1-2 percentage points per year from 1991 to 2001 (Table D4 in Smith et al. 2006) and were linearly extrapolated from 2002 (67 percent wood and 34 percent paper deposition) to 2010 (65 percent wood and 30 percent paper deposition). Approximately 23 percent of wood and 56 percent of paper entering landfill storage is estimated to decay with a half-life of 14 years (Table 9) and will therefore be 99.99 percent decayed by year 100. The nondegradable portion of landfill C (mostly lignin or inaccessible cellulose) was considered for the purposes of this analysis to be a permanent sink of C. For the landfill C fraction that decays, 50 percent by molar mass is assumed to be converted to CO_2 and 50 percent to CH_4 in anaerobic conditions (NCASI 2004). We assumed 10 percent of the landfill methane was chemically oxidized or converted by bacteria to CO_2 as it travels through the landfill soil cover (Liptay et al. 1998, USEPA 2002), although recent literature suggests this estimate is low (mean of 36.5 percent for 42 studies reviewed by Chantona et al. 2009). Based on national estimates (USEPA 2002), we assumed that 49 percent of CH4 landfill gas is produced at landfills with gas collection systems with 75 percent collection efficiency, suggesting an effective national capture rate of 36.75 percent. Approximately 49 percent of CH_4 captured (18 percent of total) is burned for energy and the remainder is flared without energy capture (Fig. 2). When burned, CH_4 is converted back to CO_2, and is therefore considered a neutral GHG emission.

Moles of landfill C transferred to atmospheric CH_4 were accounted for within CO_T and used to later calculate the CO_2 equivalent (CO_2e) mass of gas released to the atmosphere. Mass of C transferred to CH_4 gas equates to 16/12 because there are 12 g/mole of C and 16 g/mole of CH_4. CH_4 gas has a global warming potential of 25 when measured over 100 years, therefore 1 unit of landfill C released as CH_4 would create (16/12) x 25 units of CO_2e in the atmosphere. In the atmosphere, CH_4 reacts with ^-OH radicals to create CO_2 and H_2O vapor. CH_4 has a large effect for a brief period with a net lifetime of 12 years in the atmosphere and a half-life of 7 years assuming OH radicals are readily available. Because of this difference in effect and time period, the time-integrated radiative forcing effect of CH_4 compared to CO_2 is 72 over a 20-year time period and 25 over a 100-year period (IPCC 2007). For all simulations presented here, we assume a 100-year accounting period for CH_4. At 101 years post-CH4 release, the additive GHG warming impact of this CH_4 is assumed to be neutralized. We calculated energy produced from CH_4 capture by multiplying mass by its energy potential (15.47 kWh/kg) by the plants estimated predelivered energy conversion efficiency. Energy conversion efficiency is defined here as the fraction of energy in the feedstock to the power plant that is delivered to the grid. No clear estimates for energy conversion efficiency of methane in landfill gas collection facilities were found, so 37 percent was assumed based on willow biomass feedstock gasifier plant values reported by Mann and Spath (1997). This parameter can be adjusted in ForGATE in worksheet **Landfill**. Energy produced from CH_4 was used to calculate the avoided emission potential of displacing coal and natural gas sources using methods described for wood feedstock-based energy in the following section.

Energy Capture from Wood and Avoided Emission Potential

We calculated power plant energy yield from wood (harvest residues, roundwood wood and bark, and wood waste) using:

$$Energy_S = 2C * HHV_S * Eff \qquad [1]$$

where

$Energy$ = total energy produced at plant gate for distribution,

C = carbon stored in wood multiplied by 2 to convert mass of C to oven-dry biomass feedstock,

HHV = higher heating value of tree species s wood or bark based on Ince (1977), and

Eff = energy conversion efficiency of feedstock.

For wood waste delivered to landfills, an average species HHV of 20 gigajoules per oven dried tonne GJ/ODT (ranges from 17.66-22.22; Ince 1977) was used. The energy plant was assumed to be a gasifier combined-cycle system with a feedstock Eff (higher heating value basis) of 37 percent (Mann and Spath 1997). This Eff is based on green willow feedstock, and we assumed here that it would remain similar for different species green wood residues and roundwood. However, we would expect much higher Eff for use of wood waste, with comparatively lower wood green moisture content (15-20 percent) than green (40-200 percent) feedstock, and therefore reduced thermal energy loss from water vapor during gasification. All energy conversion efficiency assumptions in ForGATE can be adjusted by the user under worksheet **Mill** and **Landfill**.

Global Warming Index (GWI) values for alternative modes of electricity generation (e.g., willow biomass gasification, coal, natural gas, wind, solar, hydro) were based on life cycle assessment and environmental impact literature compiled by Spitzley and Keoleian (2004). Total life cycle global warming potential index (g CO_2 equivalent/kWh) includes cradle to gate primary and upstream emissions but does not include distribution or use emissions or energy loss during distribution. For studies compiled, GWI for most renewable-based energy sources (solar, hydro, willow biomass gasification) and nuclear energy ranged from 19.0-66.3 g CO_2e/kWh, with willow biomass indices for three studies ranging from 38.9-52.8 g CO_2e/kWh. Wind power had the lowest GWI, ranging from 1.71-2.51 g CO_2e/kWh (two studies), while coal or coal/biomass blend (758-1040 g CO_2e/kWh; six studies) and natural gas (504 g CO_2e/kWh; one study) had the highest. By using the difference in mean GWI between biomass and alternative energy sources in combination with the amount of energy produced for distribution at the gasifier from wood-based feedstock, we calculated GHG emissions that could be avoided by substituting coal and natural gas energy sources for wood. We lacked life cycle assessment data for landfill methane capture and energy production; therefore we assumed the landfill methane capture plant would yield the same GWI and Eff as the willow biomass gasifier. This, however, is a conservative assumption. We would expect GWI values to be lower for landfill energy production than for a gasifier, since many upstream plant emissions can be excluded (capture systems and landfills will exist and operate regardless of whether they produce energy) and the energy conversion efficiency of methane compared to biomass should be higher (less heat efficiency losses as no drying of wet biomass feedstock is required). These assumptions can be altered in ForGATE under worksheet **Landfill**.

Carbon Retention Yields

One unit of C for each roundwood product was simulated in CO_T through manufacturing, use, and disposal for 300 years, allowing temporal C storage in wood products and landfill pools as well as CH_4 released to the atmosphere to be calculated and expressed proportionally to the amount of roundwood C entering the CO_T simulation at time 0 (Fig. 4). Proportional C retention in use and in landfills predicted by CO_T were within 1 percent and 5 percent, respectively, of C storage at 100 years when compared to storage levels reported in Table 1.6 in Smith et al. (2006). In all cases, landfill C storage was slightly lower than reported by Smith et al. (2006) because percentage of wood and paper waste deposition extrapolated for 2010 was approximately 5 percent less than deposition proportions used by Smith. C retention yields from CO_T simulation results can be saved in a text file (comma separated values) or Microsoft Access® database. The yield tables detail the life cycle of C storage in specific wood product pools in each year of the simulation and are reported separately for each roundwood product input.

This wood product C retention yield table is loaded at runtime and intersected with stand-level quantities of roundwood products removed in treatments scheduled in FVS, such as amount of SW sawtimber C harvested in 2021.

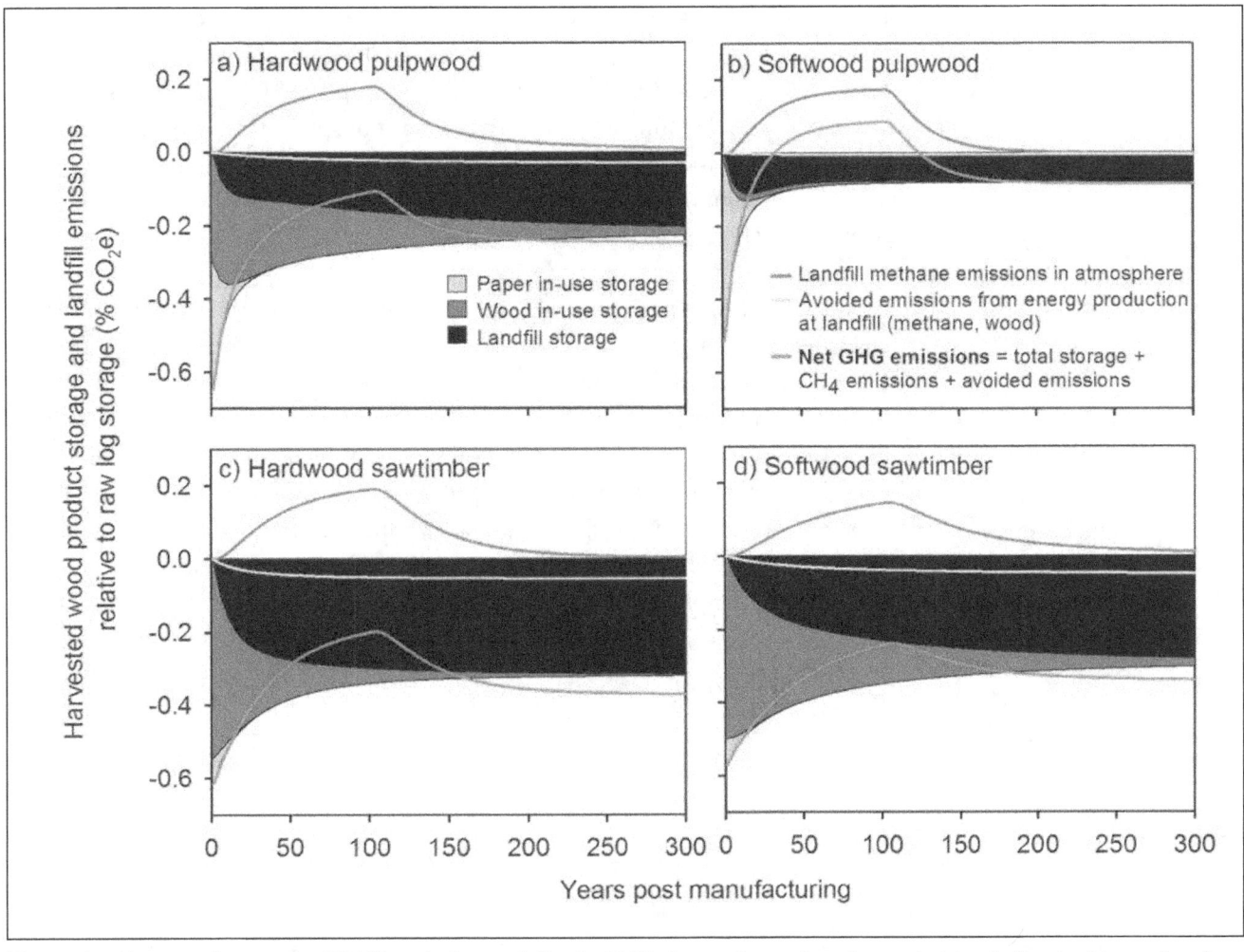

Figure 4.—Net greenhouse gas (GHG) emissions relative to GHG storage in raw logs harvested (excluding bark) as a function of total paper, wood, and landfill storage (calibrated using Smith et al. 2006) plus landfill CH_4 emissions (NCASI 2004, USEPA 2002) and landfill-avoided emissions. Positive values indicate emissions to the atmosphere, while negative values denote GHG retention of wood product in use and landfill or avoided emissions. For this example, the landfill facility(s) is assumed to be offsetting the use of natural gas with wood waste and [or] CH_4 for energy production (offset potential = 500 g CO_2e/ kWh). Effect of CH_4 on atmospheric warming is discounted to zero after 100 years from the time it was released, because we assumed a GHG warming potential of 25 for CH_4 on a 100 year GHG accounting basis (Forster 2007).

By knowing how much C was harvested in each year in each subplot and the postharvest proportional storage of C in product types (e.g., single family homes), we summarized stand- or forest-level C stock inventory reports for wood product pools.

CO_T was also used to calculate cumulative 1) landfill CH_4 emissions and energy production; 2) finished structural wood (OSB, lumber, plywood) mass for later estimation of displaced emissions from using wood products over more fossil fuel-intensive alternatives such as steel and concrete; and 3) energy and avoided emission potential of biomass removed from stands (pulpwood, tops, and branches) or collected as waste at landfills. By tracking C storage in wood products, landfill CH_4 emissions to the atmosphere, and avoided landfill emissions from waste wood use and CH_4 energy capture, we estimated net CO_2e emissions (net of methane GWP effects) potential for each roundwood product over 300 years (Fig. 4).

CO_T can be used to add and track new pool inputs as a function of other pool sink-to-source transitions. For example, mill emissions can be tracked as a function of the mass of C stored in HW sawtimber that is transferred to HW lumber. Users can define new pools such as transport emissions and force CO_T to accumulate transport emissions in this new pool by associating a transport emission factor with the amount of roundwood transported from one pool to another (forest to primary mill to secondary mill). Transport and wood processing emission factors are calculated using a number of forest sector life cycle assessments compiled from the literature, as explained in the following section.

FOREST SECTOR GREENHOUSE GAS EMISSIONS

Forest sector emission sources that were inventoried in ForGATE included: 1) harvest, 2) wood transport to and between manufacturing facilities, and 3) manufacturing raw wood into finished products (Fig. 5). Emission factors (CO_2e/unit of product handled) for each category was estimated using available machine productivity and fossil fuel emission rates and life cycle inventory and assessment literature from across North America, with preference for studies conducted in the northeast. The intent was to capture all meaningful emissions associated with the production of finished forest products that may influence forest management decisions. The life cycle inventory boundary excluded emissions from planting, site-preparation, or other non-harvest silviculture. Emissions associated with harvest machine manufacturing or floating, road construction, forest office buildings, mill construction, and emissions from transport of personnel to and from work were also excluded because infrastructure construction emissions are generally considered insignificant relative to the lifetime of infrastructure operating emissions (Eberle et al. 2007).

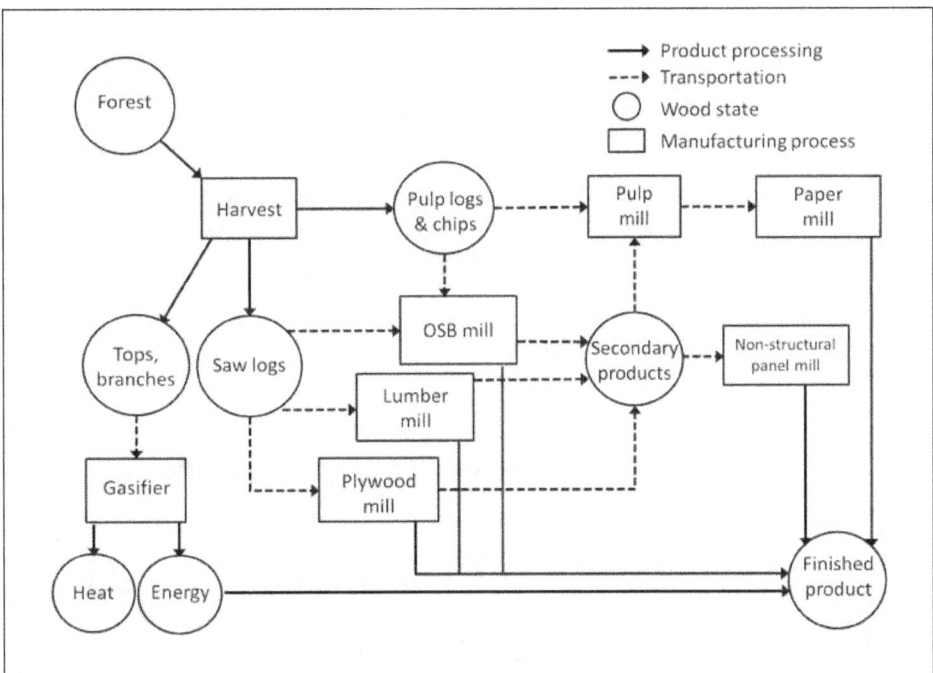

Figure 5.—A schematic overview of wood flow through various processes accounted for in ForGATE. Circles represent intermediate or final products, rectangles represent emissions from activities (harvest, manufacturing, or energy conversion), and dashed lines represent transportation emissions to and between manufacturing facilities.

Harvest and Transport

CO_2e emitted per unit of roundwood harvested is largely a function of machine fuel consumption and productivity which depends on machine type and stand conditions (FPInovation 2005). Harvest system emission factors (kg CO_2e/m^3 of roundwood produced) for two harvest systems are presented in Table 11 and include: 1) cut-to-length (harvester and forwarder), and 2) full tree (feller buncher, grapple skidder, delimber, and slasher). Upstream emissions to refine and transport the diesel were also included (0.058 kg CO_2e/l; Deluchi 1991). Emission factors for the harvester, feller buncher, delimber, and slasher were estimated using:

$$\frac{kg \; CO_2 e}{m^3} = \sum_{i=0}^{n} \left(\frac{f}{ax^b}\right)_i 3.794 \qquad [2]$$

and for the forwarder and grapple skidder using:

$$\frac{kg \; CO_2 e}{m^3} = \sum_{i=0}^{n} \left(\frac{f}{a+by}\right)_i 3.794 \qquad [3]$$

where

f = fuel consumption rate in liters per productive machine hour (pmh),

a and b = specific productivity (m^3/pmh) parameters for machine i,

x = mean stand-level m^3/tree,

y = mean skidding distance (m), and

3.794 = kg of CO_2e emitted per liter of diesel combusted (IPCC 2006a).

Table 11.—Harvest machine productivity parameters (FPInovation 2005) for equations 2 and 3 and resulting estimates of direct diesel consumption and CO_2e emissions/m^3 harvested

Machine	Parameters			Diesel consumption (L/m^3) [a]	Emission factor (kg CO_2e/ m^3) [a]
	a	b	f		
Single tree harvest system					
Log Max 7000 Head harvester	38.77	0.6	20	1.61	6.11
JD 8 wheel drive 14 tonne forwarder	26.65	-0.07	14	0.46	1.75
Total				2.07	7.86
Full tree harvest system					
1255 Gilbert Head feller buncher	102.66	0.46	32	0.75	2.83
JD 648 G grapple skidder	431.7	-0.54	24	0.02	0.08
Denharco de-Limber	70.56	0.57	18	0.75	2.85
Hahn 892 slasher	28.86	0.15	20	0.92	3.49
Total				2.44	9.25

[a] Diesel emission rate = 3.794 kg CO_2e/L (Waldron et al. 2006), stand-level average merchantable tree volume = 0.15 m^3/tree, and skid distance = 300 m for all calculations.

CO_2e emitted per weight (expressed here as t C) of raw materials transported from forest or from a different processing facility was derived using:

$$\frac{kg\ CO_2e}{tC} = \frac{\frac{d}{s}*f*3.46}{w} \quad [4]$$

where

d = total return distance (km),

s = mean travel speed (km/h),

w = t C transported per load, and

3.46 = kg CO_2e produced per liter of diesel consumed for on-road transport (IPCC 2006a).

Note that IPCC (2006a) assumes CO_2e emissions per liter of diesel combusted are lower for on-road transport compared to harvesting machines and mills as a result of emission controls (e.g., catalytic converters). For all transport calculations, we assumed a mean return distance of 160 km, travel speed of 70 km/h, and fuel consumption of 55 L/h (Gingras and Favreau 1996) for roundwood and 40 L/h (Klawer 1995) for secondary product such as tops and branches, chips, and wood waste (Table 12). Transport emissions resulting from delivery of secondary products to downstream processing facilities (e.g., lumber shavings to medium density fiberboard mills and pulp to paper mills) were also tracked (Fig. 5). Transport emissions of finished products to market were excluded.

Table 12.—Roadside-to-mill and mill-to-mill transport emission factors expressed as t CO_2e emitted per t C transported, calculated using equation 4 assuming a 160 km return distance, 70 km/hr travel speed, and 2.29 hr total travel time

	Payload [a] (t wet biomass)	Diesel burn rate (L/h) [b]	Diesel burned per load (L)	Emission factors [c]		Source
				t CO_2e/load	t CO_2e per t C transported [a]	
Roadside to mill	38	55	125.71	0.435	0.0458	Gingras and Farveau 1996
Mill to mill	30	40	91.43	0.316	0.0422	Klawer 1995

[a] t C transported per load of green biomass was determined by multiplying mass of wet biomass by 50% moisture content (on a wet basis fresh green wood has a moisture content of 35-60% depending on species; Ragland and Aerts 1991) and the mean dry biomass C content of 50% (IPCC 2003).
[b] Consumption of diesel fuel per machine hour.
[c] Emissions per liter of diesel were assumed to be 3.46 kg CO_2e based on mobile combustion of diesel fuel (Waldron et al. 2006).

Wood Manufacturing

Life cycle inventory (LCI) reports for mill primary inputs (electricity, resin, fuel, and roundwood) needed to manufacture different finished wood products are available from the Consortium for Research on Renewable Industrial Materials (CORRIM) for mills in the northern and southern United States. An LCI involves data collection and modeling of industrial systems using internationally recognized standards (ISO 2006) and determines environmental burdens associated with production of a specific product, such as lumber, as well as associated burdens from production of required raw materials (e.g., electricity, diesel fuel, resins). LCIs may also include expected burdens that occur over the product's life and disposal. LCIs from CORRIM used here include: softwood lumber (Puettmann et al. 2010), hardwood lumber (Bergman and Bowe 2008), softwood plywood (Wilson and Sakimoto 2005), medium density fiberboard (Wilson 2008a), particleboard (Wilson 2008b), hardwood flooring (Hubbard and Bowe 2010), OSB (Kline 2005), and phenol and urea-formaldehyde (resin) production (Wilson 2009). LCI boundaries of each study were, where possible, broken down by primary emission sources (those occurring at the mill site such as combustion of fossil fuels or wood) and secondary or upstream emissions necessary to produce raw materials (Fig. 6). Total emissions from fuels used at each mill were determined by type (e.g., diesel, natural gas) and amount of CO_2e produced from the combustion, extraction, and refining of fuels (Table 13).

Paper Manufacturing

Energy (electricity, fossil fuels) used to produce steam and to power other manufacturing processes during pulp and paper production across Canada was assessed by Francis et al. (2002; Table 14). As shown in Table 14, with integration and modernization of pulp and paper manufacturing processes, CO2e emissions can be greatly reduced. The benefits of modernization and integration come from reduced energy consumption due to improved energy efficiency between processes and utilization of energy produced from biomass and residues. For all scenarios in this report, we used energy consumption statistics from mean kraft market pulp and newsprint mills in Canada (Table 14; Fig. 7). It was assumed that energy for steam production (net of energy inputs from biomass boilers) was generated from burning fossil fuels at the mill, and that all electricity required was delivered from a generating station. Upstream emissions from production of chemicals at the pulp or paper mills were excluded due to lack of information.

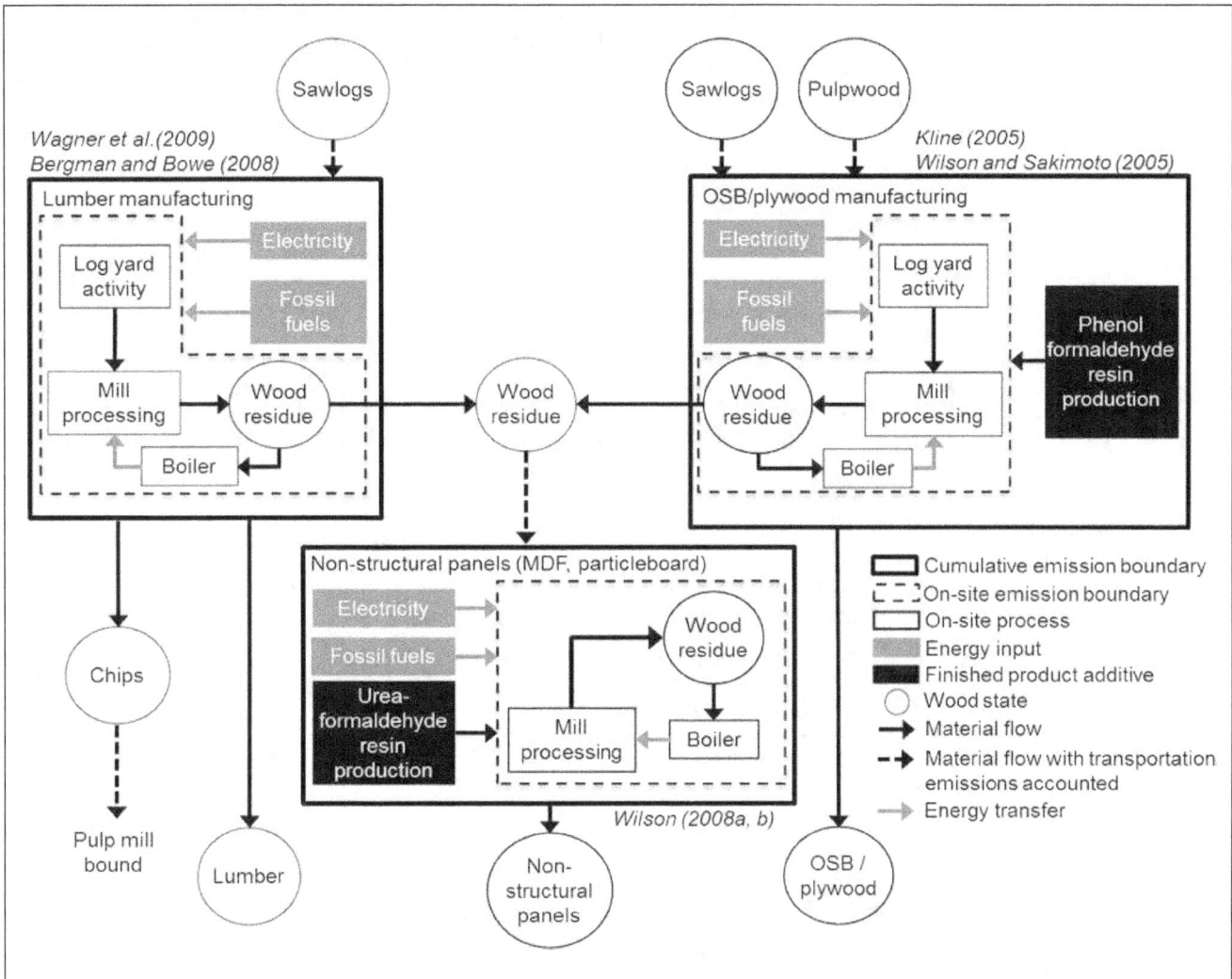

Figure 6.—Sawtimber manufacturing inputs and outputs for three categories of timber products (lumber, oriented strand board [OSB] and plywood, and nonstructural panels). Dashed rectangles represent direct mill emissions (generated on-site by burning fossil fuels), while solid rectangles represent emissions released to the atmosphere as a consequence of producing and transporting electricity, fossil fuel, and resins used in the manufacturing process. Wood harvest and transport emissions were accounted separately (Fig. 5). This figure was generalized from five separate life cycle inventories conducted by the Consortium of Research on Renewable Industrial Materials (CORRIM). References for each process are listed in the figure.

Table 13.—CO_2e emissions produced from the direct combustion (Gomez et al. 2006) and upstream (Deluchi 1991) emissions produced per gigajoule of energy created from the use of different fuel types

Fuel type	Emissions (kg CO_2e/GJ)	
	Combustion	Upstream [a]
Natural gas	56.2	10.5
Diesel fuel	74.3	15.1
Coal	95.0	8.6
Gasoline	69.3	20.1
Propane	63.1	9.4

[a] Emissions to extract and transport a specific fuel type to an end user.

Table 14.—Pulp and paper mill energy requirements for steam production and manufacturing processes per air-dried tonne of product produced (Francis et al. 2002). These required energy inputs are net of energy and steam produced at the mill from biomass boilers.

Product	Steam (GJ/t)	Electricity (kWh/t)
Kraft market pulp [a]	5.99	272
Newsprint [a]	4.46	2850
Modern pulp mill	1.2	-17
Modern newsprint mill	4.4	330
Integrated pulp and newsprint mill	0.8	2430

[a] The manufacturing processes to produce these products were used to parameterize paper product manufacturing in ForGATE.

Manufacturing Energy and Emissions Factors

The matrix of on-site fuels (diesel, natural gas, propane, heavy oil) and on-site or off-site electricity sources (coal, natural gas, nuclear, or renewable) used by a manufacturing facility can dominate the GHG emission profile of an LCI. Each CORRIM LCI study was analyzed, where possible, to determine the amount of electricity, fuel, resins, and primary wood inputs required to make one unit of finished forest product (Table 15). We were then able to calculate total manufacturing emissions as a function of mill finished products produced as well as for alternate scenarios of mill energy sources used.

Tonnes of C stored per unit of finished product were determined based on data and methods in Smith et al. (2006). By knowing the amount of C stored per unit of finished product and the associated emissions or energy required to produce one unit of finished product, we calculated the amount of on-site and upstream mill emissions generated and the energy required to produce one t C stored in each finished product (Table 15). CO_2e emissions, electrical consumption, and resin requirements for nonstructural panels in Table 15 were based on the mean

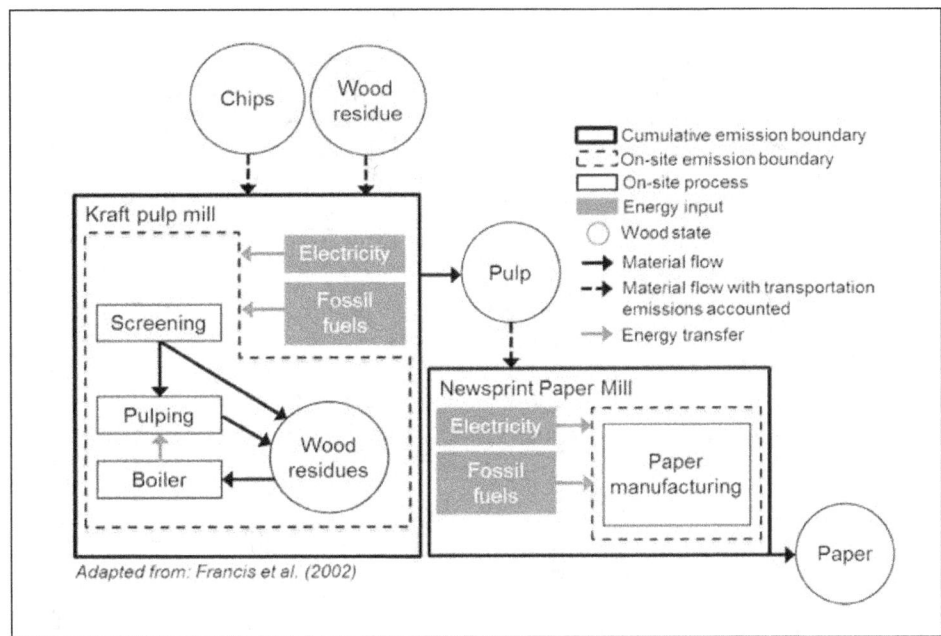

Figure 7.—Kraft pulp and newsprint paper manufacturing process generalized from Francis et al. (2002). Dashed rectangles identify direct mill emissions generated on-site by burning fossil fuels. Harvest and transport emissions were accounted separately (Fig. 5). Upstream emissions released to the atmosphere as a consequence of producing and/or transporting electricity and fossil fuels used in the manufacturing process were accounted separately from on-site emissions. Upstream emissions from production and transport of chemicals required during paper manufacturing were excluded from this study due to lack of available information.

values of medium-density fiberboard and particleboard. On-site CO_2e emissions reported for OSB, nonstructural panels, and plywood excluded upstream emissions from the production of resins (phenol and urea-formaldehyde). Using an LCI for resin production (Wilson 2009), we included expected upstream CO_2e emissions and electricity consumption for producing the resin required for OSB (0.034 kg CO_2e/m^3 and 0.068 kWh/m^3), nonstructural panels (0.108 kg CO_2e/m^3 and 0.223 kWh/m^3), and plywood (0.014 kg CO_2e/m^3 and 0.029 kWh/m^3).

Total mill emissions and energy requirements to process roundwood products from the forest were calculated by using the proportion of C transferred from log products into various finished products (Fig. 2) in combination with the mill emission and energy requirement factors in Table 15. These factors and calculations were compiled in the COT model (see the carbon accounting section) and used in combination with FVS tree list projections to calculate total stand-level mill emissions and energy requirements for the four log products (SW and HW pulpwood and SW and HW sawtimber) harvested for each simulation iteration. ForGATE users can modify assumptions about the rate of fuel and grid

Table 15.—Energy requirements and CO$_2$e emissions released per unit of finished product produced from several mill types

Finished product	Product unit	Storage (t C/unit)	Mill emission outputs or energy requirements					Emissions (t CO$_2$e/t C)	Electricity (kWh/t C)	Steam (GJ/t C)	Reference
			On-site		Upstream [d]						
			Emissions[a] (kg CO$_2$e)	Steam (GJ)	Emissions (kg CO$_2$e)	Electricity (kWh)	Resin (kg CO$_2$e)				
Softwood Lumber	m³	0.264	54.04	-	1.12	62	-	0.209	234.49	-	Wagner et al. 2009
Hardwood Lumber	m³	0.324	46.60	-	9.88	165	-	0.174	508.95	-	Bergman and Bowe. 2008
Plywood [b]	m³	0.267	6.17	-	3.76	156	0.01	0.037	584.93	-	Wilson and Sakimoto 2005
OSB	m³	0.311	52.06	-	7.55	58	0.03	0.192	186.62	-	Kline 2005
Nonstructural Panels [b]	m³	0.327	70.36	-	12.17	277	0.11	0.253	848.13	-	Wilson 2008a,b
Kraft Market Pulp [c]	t	0.496	-	5.99	-	272	-	-	548.39	12.08	Francis et al. 2002
Newsprint [c]	t	0.496	-	4.46	-	2850	-	-	5745.97	8.99	Francis et al. 2002

[a] Excludes energy requirements met from biogenic sources (biomass boilers).

[b] Values for the production of medium density fiberboard and particleboard were averaged together to approximate emissions, electrical consumption and resin requirements for the nonstructural panels.

[c] Excludes emissions to create and transport pulp and paper manufacturing chemicals.

[d] Emissions produced in the manufacturing of products and resources off-site.

electricity emissions expected for their facilities and jurisdiction. For example, grid electricity in Maine may be generated from hydro and natural gas, while electricity in Vermont may be generated primarily from coal. Therefore, a similar manufacturing facility in different locations may have very different GHG profiles (Fig. 8).

A comparison of manufacturing emissions for wood products in Canada versus the United States is available in Figure 8.1 in Natural Resources Canada (2010). In addition, Table 8.1 in the same report provides comparisons with jurisdictions in South America and Europe. Emission values reported from these sources are comparable to values reported in Table 15. State-specific CO_2e emissions for electricity generation can be calculated using EIA (2001) and Spitzley and Keoleian (2004), while CO_2e emissions from production and extraction of different fuel types can be obtained from Table 13 and Environment Canada (2008). Additional LCIs for wood products produced in Canada are available from the Athena Institute (2008a, b; 2009a, b, c).

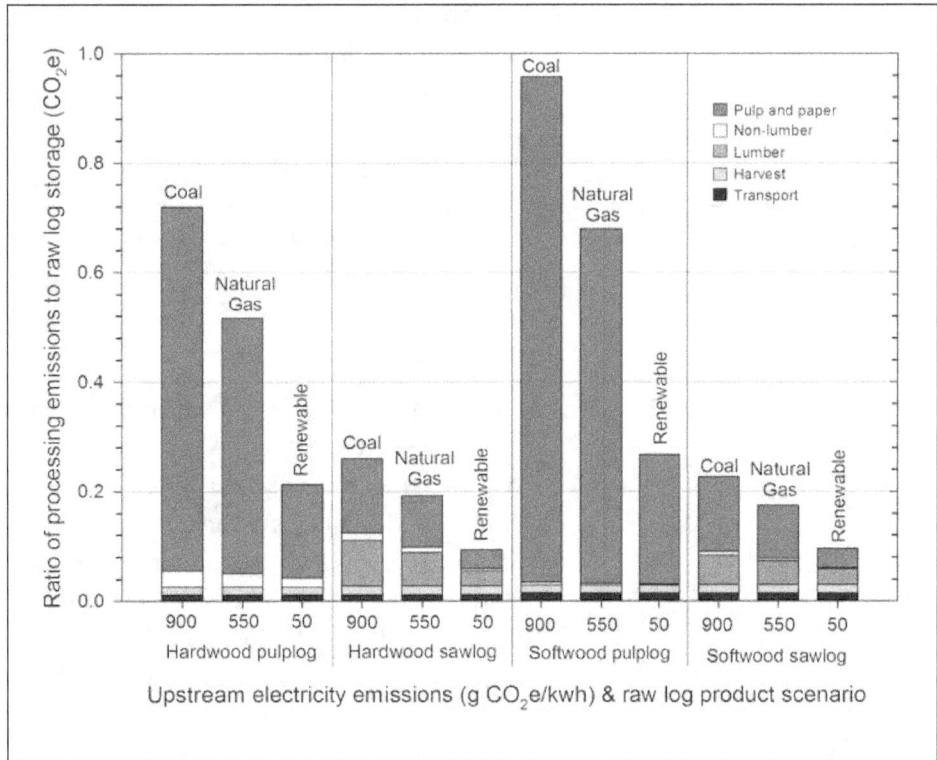

Figure 8.—Harvest (Table 11), transport (Table 12), and mill (Table 15) CO_2e emissions (including upstream) to extract and process four log products (softwood, hardwood x pulplog, sawlog) relative to log CO_2e storage (excluding bark) as a function of: 1) finished products produced from raw products (Smith et al. 2006); and 2) three upstream electricity generation emission rate assumptions (coal [900 g CO_2e/kWh]; natural gas [550 g CO_2e/kWh]; and renewable [50 g CO_2e/kWh]) generalized from Spitzley and Keoleian (2004). For pulp and paper mills in this example, natural gas was assumed to be used to produce steam where required (Table 15).

LIMITATIONS AND SUGGESTED IMPROVEMENTS

While ForGATE can provide GHG emission comparisons among a large array of potential offset projects and GHG accounting parameter values, it lacks sufficient forest inventory, management, and manufacturing resolution to be used for actual C offset project reporting where credits must be verified on the ground and for specific operations or mills. For example, emission assumptions for pulp and paper manufacturing were based on average newsprint mills in Canada, rather than average mills in Maine. While mill electricity and fuel source information can be adjusted to better reflect upstream emissions for Maine, ForGATE is unlikely to capture the true life cycle inventory of emissions for a given operation. Following exploration of C offset projects in ForGATE, those deemed worthy of further consideration should be further assessed using:

1) an integrated forest estate management-C modeling framework that provides operational planning resolution of forest growth and succession following treatments (e.g., Smith and Heath 2004; Hennigar et al. 2008; Kurz et al. 2009),

2) a life cycle inventory of all upstream and on-site emissions by harvest and transport system and by each mill that consumes wood from lands under the scope of the project boundary, and finally,

3) a forest products model that accurately reflects products produced, market destinations, and expected use and disposal pathways.

Forest Carbon Modeling

All emissions in ForGATE are either directly or indirectly driven by forest growth and yield projections. Although FVS-NE was constrained to project stands within the live biomass and basal area bounds of current inventory conditions in Maine (see the model calibration section), little effort was made to validate model growth or mortality rates or growth response for treated stands. In future versions, more effort should be directed to this area as recommended by Saunders et al. (2008). Recalibration of ForGATE for Maine is also recommended once the Acadian FVS variant is released and validated (expected in 2012).

While dead organic matter (DOM) pools (snags, forest floor, belowground soil) were modeled in FVS-NE and represented in ForGATE, the Forest Inventory and Analysis plot data (Phase 2 plots) used as input to the model lacked estimates of DOM. Therefore, starting steady state inventory levels of DOM pools in

ForGATE are undoubtedly underestimated, and hence sequestration in these pools projected over time is likely overestimated. DOM pool initialization could be greatly improved by utilizing Phase 3 FIA plots which do contain estimates of biomass and carbon levels in these pools for each inventory plot.

Forest Product Carbon Modeling

Pulpwood and sawtimber volumes were estimated directly from FVS-NE. Because product volume calculations in FVS-NE are based primarily on tree taper and, in this study, lacked operational realities of reduced product grades or market forces, estimates should be viewed as potential volumes rather than actual volumes. For this same reason, pulp-timber volume ratios are also probably underestimated. In future work, annual wood processing reports, available from the Maine Forest Service, could be used to better adjust or validate FVS-NE product proportions.

Both raw and finished product output proportions have a large effect on resulting forest product C storage profiles and forest sector emissions. Proportions of finished forest product types and end-use product markets for Maine are based on northeast averages compiled by Smith et al. (2006), which are also used in current U.S. forest product accounting standards. Estimates likely vary from state to state and could be customized for Maine.

Methane emissions from forest product decay in landfills are a very significant source of GHG relative to the C storage potential of forest products. Based on national estimates (USEPA 2002), we assumed that 49 percent of landfill methane gas is produced at landfills with gas collection systems. Methane capture efficiencies at landfills, however, have been increasing steadily from 10 percent since the 1990s (USEPA 2010). It is likely that this trend will continue given increased pressure to reduce emissions and because methane capture at landfills is considered a low cost carbon offset project. Incorporating a time-dependent increase in methane capture from present levels to 80-90 percent by 2020 (linearly interpolated) within the forest product model would have significant influence on reducing forest product related emissions.

Forest Sector Emissions

A large number of geographically disparate life cycle inventory and analysis studies, mostly from Consortium for Research on Renewable Industrial Materials, were used to estimate emissions from various manufacturing facilities. We factored out electricity and fuel source assumptions where possible, but mill configurations and energy requirements should be validated against facilities in Maine. Of the pulp and paper facility emission inventories reviewed, fossil fuel and electricity inputs varied up to ten fold. Given the overwhelming influence of pulp and paper emissions relative to all other sector emission sources, explicit calibration of the ratio of types and energy requirements of Maine's pulp and paper facilities would greatly improve projected manufacturing emission rates in ForGATE which are currently based on mean values from studies reviewed across North America.

ACKNOWLEDGMENTS

We would like to thank the following individuals who provided input at various stages of the development of this tool: John Hagan, Manomet Center for Conservation Sciences; Tom Charles, Maine Bureau of Public Lands; David Saah, Spatial Informatics Group; Jeremy Wilson, University of Maine; Aaron Weiskittel, University of Maine; and Richard Birdsey, U.S. Forest Service, Northern Research Station.

This work is supported by funding from the U.S. Forest Service Global Change Program, the Manomet Center for Conservation Sciences, and the University of New Brunswick. The work upon which this project is based was also funded in part through a grant awarded by the Wood Education and Resource Center, Northeastern Area State and Private Forestry, U.S. Forest Service.

LITERATURE CITED

Arner, S.L.; Woudenberg, S.; Waters, S.; Vissage, J.; MacLean, C.; Thompson, M.; Hansen, M. 2001. **National algorithm for determining stocking class, stand size class, and forest type for Forest Inventory and Analysis plots.** Newtown Square, PA: U.S. Department of Agriculture, Forest Service, Northeastern Research Station; internal report. 12 p. Available at http://www. fs.fed.us/fmsc/ftp/fvs/docs/gtr/Arner2001.pdf. (Accessed July 20, 2011).

Athena Institute. 2008a. **A cradle-to-gate life cycle assessment of Canadian oriented strand board sheathing.** Ottawa, ON: Athena Sustainable Materials Institute; final report. 87 p. Available at http://www.athenasmi.org/ publications/docs/CIPEC_Canadian_OSB_LCA_final_report.pdf. (Accessed September 3, 2010).

Athena Institute. 2008b. **A cradle-to-gate life cycle assessment of Canadian softwood plywood sheathing.** Ottawa, ON: Athena Sustainable Materials Institute; final report. 86 p. Available at http://www.athenasmi.ca/ publications/docs/CIPEC_Canadian_Plywood_LCA_Final_Report.pdf. (Accessed September 3, 2010).

Athena Institute. 2009a. **A cradle-to-gate life cycle assessment of Canadian medium density fiberboard (MDF).** Ottawa, ON: Athena Sustainable Materials Institute; final report. 95 p. Available at http://www.athenasmi.org/ publications/docs/CIPEC_Canadian_MDF_LCA_final_report.pdf. (Accessed September 3, 2010).

Athena Institute. 2009b. **A cradle-to-gate life cycle assessment of Canadian particleboard.** Ottawa, ON: Athena Sustainable Materials Institute; final report. 93 p. Available at http://www.athenasmi.org/publications/ docs/CIPEC_Canadian_Particleboard_LCA_final_report_20090731.pdf. (Accessed September 3, 2010).

Athena Institute. 2009c. **A cradle-to-gate life cycle assessment of Canadian softwood lumber.** Ottawa, ON: Athena Sustainable Materials Institute; final report. 143 p. Available at http://www.athenasmi.org/publications/docs/ CIPEC_Lumber_LCA_Final_Report.pdf. (Accessed September 3, 2010).

Bankowski, J.; Dey, D.; Boysen, E.; Woods, M.; Rice, J. 1996. **Validation of NE-TWIGS for tolerant hardwood stands in Ontario.** Sault Ste. Marie, ON: Ontario Ministry of Natural Resources. Forest Research Information Paper No. 103. 21 p.

Bergman, R.D.; Bowe, S.A. 2008. **Life-cycle inventory of hardwood lumber manufacturing in the Northeast and Northcentral United States: module C.** Seattle, WA: Consortium for Research on Renewable Industrial Materials (CORRIM). Phase II Final Report. 48 p.

Bilek, E.M.; Becker, P.; MacAbee, T. 2009. **CVal: a spreadsheet tool to evaluate the direct benefits and costs of carbon sequestration contracts for managed forests.** Gen. Tech. Rep. FPL-180. Madison, WI: U.S. Department of Agriculture, Forest Service, Forest Products Laboratory. 27 p.

Briedis, J.; Wilson, J.; Benjamin, J.; Wagner, R. 2011. **Biomass retention following whole-tree, energy-wood harvest in central Maine: compliance to five state guidelines.** Biomass and Bioenergy. 35: 3552-3560.

Brissette, J.C. 1996. **Effects of intensity and frequency of harvesting on abundance, stocking, and composition, of natural regeneration in the Acadian Forest of eastern North America.** Silva Fennica. 30: 301-314.

Carle, J.-F. 2011. **Integrated planning of timber harvest and bioenergy production for large forest areas: a case study for Crown land of New Brunswick.** MScF Thesis, University of New Brunswick, Fredericton, NB. 92 p.

Chantona, J.P.; Powelsona, D.K.; Green, R.B. 2009. **Methane oxidation in landfill cover soils, is a 10% default value reasonable?** Journal of Environmental Quality. 38: 654-663.

Climate Action Reserve. 2010. **Forest project protocol: version 3.1 (October 22, 2009).** Los Angeles, CA: Climate Action Reserve. Available at http://www.climateactionreserve.org/how/protocols/adopted/forest/development. (Accessed June 3, 2010).

Cormier, D.; Ryans, M. 2006. **The Bios model for estimating forest biomass supply and costs.** Pointe-Claire, QC: Forest Engineering Research Institute of Canada (FERIC); Internal Report IR-2006-05-23. 32 p.

Crookston, N.L. 1997. **Suppose: an interface to the Forest Vegetation Simulator.** In: Teck, R.; Moeur, M.; Adams, J., comps. Proceedings: Forest Vegetation Simulator conference; 1997 Feb. 3-7; Fort Collins, CO. Gen. Tech. Rep. INT-373. Ogden, UT: U.S. Department of Agriculture, Forest Service, Intermountain Research Station: 7-14.

Crookston, N.L.; Dixon, G.E. 2005. **The Forest Vegetation Simulator: a review of its structure, content, and applications.** Computers and Electronics in Agriculture. 49: 60-80.

Deluchi, M.A. 1991. **Emissions of greenhouse gases from the use of transportation fuels and electricity. Volume 1.** Argonne, IL: Center for Transportation Research, Argonne National Laboratory. 142 p.

Diaz, D.; Hamilton, K.; Johnson, E.; Bendana, M. 2011. **State of the forest carbon markets 2011: from canopy to currency.** Washington, DC: Ecosystem Marketplace. 93 p.

Dixon, G.E. 2002. **Essential FVS: A user's guide to the Forest Vegetation Simulator.** (Revised June 27, 2010). Fort Collins, CO: U.S. Department of Agriculture, Forest Service, Forest Management Service Center; internal report. 240 p. Available at http://www.fs.fed.us/fmsc/ftp/fvs/docs/gtr/EssentialFVS.pdf .

Dixon, G.E.; Keyser, C.E., comps. 2008. **Northeast (NE) variant overview test version – Forest Vegetation Simulator.** Rev. July 29, 2010. Fort Collins, CO: U.S. Department of Agriculture, Forest Service; internal report. 42 p. Available at http://www.fs.fed.us/fmsc/ftp/fvs/docs/overviews/nenewvar.pdf. (Accessed August 19, 2010).

Eberle, U.; Lange, A.; Dewaele, J.; Schowanek, D. 2007. **LCA study and environmental benefits for low temperature disinfection process in commercial laundry.** International Journal of Life Cycle Assessment. 12: 127-138.

Energy Information Administration (EIA). 2001. **Updated state-level greenhouse gas emission factors for electricity generation.** Washington, DC: U.S. Department of Energy. 12 p. Available at http://tonto.eia.doe.gov/ftproot/environment/e-supdoc.pdf. (Accessed August 23, 2010).

Environment Canada. 2008. **Canada's greenhouse gas inventory 1990-2006, greenhouse gas sources and sinks in Canada.** Ottawa, ON: Environment Canada. 620 p. Available at http://www.ec.gc.ca/Publications/default.asp?lang=En&xml=A17AECDC-E1DC-4A81-8D63-01219B2EA617. (Accessed March 30, 2010).

FPInovation. 2005. **ProVue 2005.** Available at http://www.feric.ca/en/index.cfm?objectid=825F91A3-A960-FD3B-E1D7FB47BA9645B0. (Accessed Sept. 20, 2009).

Forster, P.; Ramaswamy, V.; Artaxo, P. [et al.]. 2007. **Changes in atmospheric constituents and in radiative forcing.** In: Solomon, S.; Qin, D.; Manning, M. [et al.], eds. Climate change 2007: the physical science basis. contribution of working group I to the fourth assessment report of the Intergovernmental Panel on Climate Change. Cambridge, UK; New York, NY: Cambridge University Press: 129-234. Chap. 2. Available at http://www.ipcc.ch/pdf/assessment-report/ar4/wg1/ar4-wg1-chapter2.pdf. [Date accessed unknown].

Francis, D.W.; Towers, M.T.; Browne, T.C. 2002. **Energy cost reduction in the pulp and paper industry – and energy benchmarking perspective.** Ottawa, ON: The Office of Energy Efficiency of Natural Resources Canada. 28 p. Available at http://oee.nrcan.gc.ca/publications/infosource/pub/cipec/pulp-paper-industry/pdf/pulp-paper-industry.pdf. (Accessed April 3, 2010).

Galik, C.S.; Baker, J.S.; Grinelle, J.L. 2009a. **Transaction costs and forest management carbon offset potential.** Durham, NC: Climate Change Policy Partnership-Duke University. 15 p. Available at: http://www.nicholas.duke.edu/ccpp/ccpp_pdfs/transaction.07.09.pdf. (Accessed Oct. 2, 2012).

Galik, C.S.; Mobley, M.L.; Richter, D. 2009b. **A virtual "field test" of forest management carbon offset protocols: the influence of accounting.** Mitigation and Adaptation Strategies for Global Change. 14: 677-690.

Gingras, J.F.; Favreau, J. 1996. **Comparative cost analysis of integrated harvesting and delivery of roundwood and forest biomass.** Pointe-Claire, QC: Forest Engineering Research Institute of Canada (FERIC). Special Report No. SR-111. 23 p.

Gomez, D.R.; Watterson, J.D.; Americano, B.B. [et al.]. 2006. **Stationary combustion.** In: Eggleston, S.; Buendia, L.; Miwa, K.; Ngara, T.; Kiyoto, T., editors. 2006 IPCC guidelines for national greenhouse gas inventories. Vol. 2: Energy. Hayama, Japan: Institute for Global Environmental Strategies for the IPCC: 2.1-2.47. Chap. 2. Available at http://www.ipcc-nggip.iges.or.jp/public/2006gl/vol2.html. [Date accessed unknown].

Heath, L.S.; Hansen, M.H.; Smith, J.E.; Miles, P.D.; Smith, B.W. 2009. **Investigation into calculating tree biomass and carbon in the FIADB using a biomass expansion factor approach.** In: McWilliams, W.; Moisen, G.; Czaplewski, R., comps. Forest Inventory and Analysis (FIA) Symposium 2008. October 21-23, 2008; Park City, UT. RMRS-P-56CD. Fort Collins, CO: U.S. Department of Agriculture, Forest Service, Rocky Mountain Research Station. 26 p.

Hennigar, C.R.; MacLean, D.A.; Amos-Binks, L.J. 2008. **A novel approach to optimize management strategies for carbon stored in both forests and wood products.** Forest Ecology and Management. 256: 786-797.

Hubbard, S.S.; Bowe, S.A. 2010. **A gate-to-gate life-cycle inventory of solid hardwood flooring in the eastern US.** Wood Fiber Science. 42: 79-89.

Ince, P.J. 1977. **Estimating effective heating value of wood or bark fuels at various moisture content.** Gen. Tech. Rep. FPL-13. Madison, WI: U.S. Department of Agriculture, Forest Service, Forest Products Laboratory. 9 p.

International Organization for Standardization (ISO). 2006. **International Standard 14040.** Switzerland: ISO Copyright Office. 20 p.

Jenkins, J.C.; Chojnacky, D.C.; Heath, L.S.; Birdsey, R.A. 2003. **National-scale biomass estimators for United States tree species.** Forest Science. 49: 12-35.

Kline, D. 2005. **Gate-to-gate life-cycle inventory of oriented strand board production.** Wood Fiber Science. 37: 74-84.

Klawer, P. 1995. **On-/off-highway transportation of wood chips with a TAC B-train trailer.** FERIC special report no. SR-106. Vancouver, BC: Canadian Forest Service and Alberta Land and Forest Services. 24 p.

Kurz, W.A.; Dymond, C.C.; White, T.M.; Stinson, G.; Shaw, C.H.; Rampley, G.J.; Smyth, C.; Simpson, B.N.; Neilson, E.T.; Trofymow, J.A.; Metsaranta, J.; Apps, M.J. 2009. **CBM-CFS3: a model of carbon-dynamics in forestry and land-use change implementing IPCC standards.** Ecological Modeling. 220: 480-504.

Li, R.; Weiskittel, A.R.; Kershaw, J.A. 2011. **Modeling annualized occurrence, frequency, and composition of ingrowth using mixed-effects zero-inflated models and permanent plots in the Acadian Region of North America.** Canadian Journal of Forest Research. 41: 2077-2089.

Lippke, B.; Oneil, E.; Harrison, R.; Skog, K.; Gustavsson, L.; Sathre, R. 2011. **Life-cycle impacts of forest management and wood utilization on carbon mitigation in the forest and wood products: knowns and unknowns.** Carbon Management. 2: 303-333.

Liptay, K.; Chanton, J.; Czepiel, P.; Mosher, B. 1998. **Use of stable isotopes to determine methane oxidation in landfill cover soils.** Journal of Geophysical Research. 103: 8243-8250.

Mann, M.K.; Spath, P.L. 1997. **Life cycle assessment of a biomass gasification combined-cycle system.** Golden, CO: U.S. Department of Energy, National Renewable Energy Laboratory; Report No. NREL/TP-430-23076. 160 p.

Murray, B.C.; McCarl, B.A.; Lee, H. 2004. **Estimating leakage from forest carbon sequestration programs.** Land Economics. 80: 109-124.

National Council for Air and Stream Improvement, Inc. (NCASI). 2004. **Critical review of forest products decomposition in municipal solid waste landfills.** Tech. Bul. No. 872. Research Triangle Park, NC: NCASI. 46 p.

Natural Resources Canada. 2010. **Status of energy use in the Canadian wood products sector.** Ottawa, ON: Natural Resources Canada. 74 p.

Nyland, R.D. 1998. **Selection system in northern hardwoods.** Journal of Forestry. 96: 18-21.

Penman, J.; Gytarsky, M.; Hiraishi, T. [et al.]. 2003. **Good practice guidance for land use, land-use change and forestry.** Hayama, Japan: Institute for Global Environmental Strategies for the IPCC. 632 p. Available at http://www.ipcc-nggip.iges.or.jp/public/gpglulucf/gpglulucf_contents.html. (Accessed January 3, 2008).

Puettmann, M.E.; Wagner, F.G.; Johnson, L.R. 2010. **Life cycle inventory of inland Northwest softwood lumber manufacturing.** Wood and Fiber Science. 42: 52-66.

Ragland, K.W.; Aerts, D.J. 1991. **Properties of wood for combustion analysis.** Bioresource Technology. 37: 161-168.

Ray, D.; Keyser, C.; Seymour, R.; Brissette, J. 2008. **Predicting the recruitment of established regeneration into the sapling size class following partial cutting in the Acadian Forest Region: Using long-term observations to assess the performance of FVS-NE.** In: Harvis, R.N.; Crookston, N.L., eds. Third forest vegetation simulator conference. RMRS-P-54. Fort Collins, CO: U.S. Department of Agriculture, Forest Service, Rocky Mountain Research Station: 186-200.

Reinhardt, E.; Crookston, N.L.; Rebain, S.A., eds. 2009. **The fire and fuels extension to the Forest Vegetation Simulator.** Addendum to RMRS-GTR-116. Ogden, UT: U.S. Department of Agriculture, Forest Service, Rocky Mountain Research Station. 244 p. Available at http://www.fs.fed.us/fmsc/ftp/fvs/docs/gtr/FFEaddendum.pdf. (Accessed July 2, 2010).

Saunders, M.; Wagner, R.; Seymour, R. 2008. **Thinning regimes for spruce-fir stands in the Northeastern United States and Eastern Canada.** Orono, ME: Cooperative Forestry Research Unit, University of Maine. 186 p. Available at http://www.umaine.edu/cfru/publications/PCT_FinalReport_Saunders_10.10.08.pdf. (Accessed July 13, 2011).

Schofield, D.A. 2003. **Vegetation dynamics and tree radial growth response in harvest gaps, natural gaps, and closed canopy conditions in Maine's Acadian forest.** Orono, ME: University of Maine. M.S. thesis.

Smith, J.E.; Heath, L.S. 2004. **Carbon stocks and projections on public forestlands in the United States, 1952-2040.** Environmental Management. 33: 433-442.

Smith, J.E.; Heath, L.S.; Skog, K.E.; Birdsey, R.A. 2006. **Methods for calculating forest ecosystem and harvested carbon, with standard estimates for forest types of the United States.** Gen. Tech. Rep. NE-343. Newtown Square, PA: U.S. Department of Agriculture, Forest Service, Northeast Research Station. 216 p.

Spitzley, D.V.; Keoleian, G.A. 2004. **Life cycle environmental and economic assessment of willow biomass electricity: a comparison with other renewable and non-renewable sources.** Ann Arbor, MI: Center for Sustainable Systems, University of Michigan. Report No. CSS04-05R. 71 p.

U.S. Environmental Protection Agency (USEPA). 2002. **Solid waste management and greenhouse gases: a life-cycle assessment of emissions and sinks.** 2nd ed. Washington, DC: U.S. Environmental Protection Agency; Report Number EPA530-R-02-006. Available at http://www.epa.gov/climatechange/wycd/waste/downloads/greengas.pdf. (Accessed March 30, 2010).

U.S. Environmental Protection Agency (USEPA). 2010. **Inventory of U.S. greenhouse gas emissions and sinks: 1990-2008: ANNEX 3 methodological descriptions for additional source or sink categories.** Washington, DC: U.S. Environmental Protection Agency: 292-297. Available at http://www.epa.gov/climatechange/Downloads/ghgemissions/US-GHG-Inventory-2010-Annexes.pdf. (Accessed February 25, 2012).

van der Werf, G.R.; Morton, D.C.; DeFries, R.S.; Olivier, J.G.J.; Kasibhatla, P.S.; Jackson, R.B.; Collatz, G.J.; Randerson, J.T. 2009. **CO_2 emissions from forest loss.** Nature Geoscience. 2: 737-738.

Wagner, F.; Puettmann, M.E.; Johnson, L.R. 2009. **Life cycle inventory of Inland Northwest softwood lumber manufacturing. Module B.** Seattle, WA: Consortium for Research on Renewable Industrial Materials (CORRIM). 89 p.

Waldron, C.D.; Harnisch, J.; Lucon, O. [et al.]. 2006. **Mobile combustion.** In: Eggleston, S.; Buendia, L.; Miwa, K.; Ngara, T.; Kiyoto, T., eds. 2006. IPCC guidelines for national greenhouse gas inventories. Volume 2: Energy. Hayama, Japan: Institute for Global Environmental Strategies on behalf of the IPCC: 3.1-3.78. Chap. 3. Available at http://www.ipcc-nggip.iges.or.jp/public/2006gl/pdf/2_Volume2/V2_3_Ch3_Mobile_Combustion.pdf. (Accessed October 2, 2012).

Weiskittel, A.R.; Wagner, R.G.; Seymour, R.S. 2010. **Refinement of the forest vegetation simulator, northeastern variant growth and yield model: phase 1.** In: Meyer, S.R., ed. Cooperative Forestry Research Unit: 2009 Annual Report. Orono, ME: University of Maine: 44-48. Available at http://www.umaine.edu/cfru/publications/AR_2009_web.pdf. (Accessed July 20, 2011).

Weiskittel, A.R.; Wagner, R.G.; Seymour, R.S. 2011. **Refinement of the forest vegetation simulator, northeastern variant growth and yield model: phase 2.** In: Mercier, W.J.; Nelson, A.S., eds. Cooperative Forestry Research Unit: 2010 Annual Report. Orono, ME: University of Maine: 23-30 Available at http://www.umaine.edu/cfru/publications/AR_2010_web.pdf. (Accessed July 20, 2011).

Wilson, J.B. 2008a. **Medium density fiberboard (MDF): a life-cycle inventory of manufacturing panels from resource through product. Phase II – Life cycle environmental performance of renewable building materials in the context of residential construction. Module G.** Seattle, WA: Consortium for Research on Renewable Industrial Materials (CORRIM). 50 p.

Wilson, J.B. 2008b. **Particleboard: a life-cycle inventory of manufacturing panels from resource through product. Phase II – Life cycle environmental performance of renewable building materials in the context of residential construction. Module F.** Seattle, WA: Consortium for Research on Renewable Industrial Materials (CORRIM). 49 p.

Wilson, J.B. 2009. **Resins: a life-cycle inventory of manufacturing resins used in the wood composites industry. Phase II – Life cycle environmental performance of renewable building materials in the context of residential construction. Module H.** Seattle, WA: Consortium for Research on Renewable Industrial Materials (CORRIM). 81 p.

Wilson, J.; Sakimoto, E. 2005. **Gate-to-gate life-cycle inventory of softwood plywood production.** Wood Fiber Science. 37: 58-73.

Woodbury, P.B.; Smith, J.E.; Heath, L.S. 2007. **Carbon sequestration in the U.S. forest sector from 1990 to 2010.** Forest Ecology and Management. 241: 14-27.

Woudenberg, S.W.; Conkling, B.L.; O'Connell, B.M.; LaPoint, E.B.; Turner, J.A.; Waddell, K.L. 2010. **The forest inventory and analysis database: database description and users manual version 4.0 for phase 2.** Gen. Tech. Rep. RMRS-GTR- 245. Fort Collins, CO: U.S. Department of Agriculture, Forest Service, Rocky Mountain Research Station. 336 p.

APPENDIX A

Appendix A: ForGATE Assumptions and Referenced Sources by Report Section

Section	Information/Assumption (* indicates adjustable in ForGATE)	Source
ForGATE TOOL: Background Assumptions and Calibration	No disturbances assumed	-
	No climate change assumed	-
	Once a given area is committed to a given silvicultural regime, it will remain managed under that regime forever.	-
	Calculation of current and long-term key performance indictors tracked in ForGATE	Table 1 and 2
Economics Results Worksheet	Economic calculations and assumptions*	Bilek et al. 2009; Galik et al. 2009a
FOREST INVENTORY AND STAND GROWTH MODELING	Forest inventory	Maine's current forest inventory of permanent sample plots measured from 2002-2006; Total subplots used = 6,278; Excludes non-stocked plots and plots with missing site information
	Stand model	FVS-NE; Crookston and Dixon 2005; Dixon and Keyser 2008
	Calibrated growth using FVS-NE's internal auto-growth-calibration process using periodic tree-level growth increments for the previous FIA permanent sample plot (PSP) measurement period.	Crookston and Dixon 2005
	Limited basal area for spruce-fir stand types to 50 m²/ha	Based on recommendations from Saunders et al. (2008)
	Maximum tree d.b.h. limits	Based on FIA maximum recorded species d.b.h. (95th percentile; Table 4)
	Background stem ingrowth	Li et al. (2011)
	Regeneration pulses (sprouting and new seedlings) following harvest	FVS sprouting postharvest based on Crookston and Dixon (2005); Following heavy harvest, a regeneration pulse of 1800 stems (Ray et al. 2008) was assumed to occur with species proportions reflecting preharvest stand species composition with adjustments for reduced competition for light (see text)
	Stand type classification – 96 stand types	Expert panel approach
	Silviculture prescriptions – 7 treatments	Expert panel approach; Nyland 1998; Suppose application (Crookston 1997); Text and Table 8

(Appendix A continued on next page)

Appendix A (continued): ForGATE Assumptions and Referenced Sources by Report Section

Section	Information/Assumption (* indicates adjustable in ForGATE)	Source
FOREST AND FOREST PRODUCT CARBON ACCOUNTING	Live biomass equations	Jenkins et al. 2003; Heath et al. 2009; Woudenberg et al. 2010
	Dead biomass estimates	Reinhardt et al. 2009
	Pulp and saw log volume	FVS-NE default constraints and equations; Dixon and Keyser 2008
	Recovery efficiency of bole wood harvested = 100%	-
	Recovery efficiency of tops and branches following harvest: i) 43% for softwood and ii) 67% for hardwood	Cormier and Ryans (2006); Carle (2011); Briedis et al. (2011)
	Harvested wood product (HWP) C-flow model	Hennigar et al. 2008
	Mill roundwood utilization statistics, product end use, and landfill decay rates.	Smith et al. (2006)
Disposal and Methane Emissions Assumptions	10% of methane from landfills chemically oxidized by landfill cover soils*	Liptay et al. 1998; USEPA 2002
	49% of landfills with gas collection systems with 75% collection efficiency*	USEPA 2002
	Global warming potential of CH_4 is 25 times that of CO_2 by gas mass over 100 years.	Forster et al. 2007
	Methane energy conversion efficiency*	Assumed the same as willow biomass feedstock gasifier plant reported by Mann and Spath (1997)
Energy Capture From Wood and Avoided Emission Potential	Higher heating values for wood derived from forest.	Ince (1977)
	Higher heating value of 20 GJ/ODT for wood delivered to landfill.	Based on average of species from Ince (1977)
	Wood energy conversion efficiency was assumed equal to a gasifier combined-cycle system with a feedstock conversion efficiency (higher heating value basis) of 37%*	Mann and Spath 1997
	Emissions from electricity generation*	Based on life cycle assessment and environmental impact literature compiled by Spitzley and Keoleian (2004)

(Appendix A continued on next page)

Appendix A (continued): ForGATE Assumptions and Referenced Sources by Report Section

Section	Information/Assumption (* indicates adjustable in ForGATE)	Source
FOREST SECTOR GREENHOUSE GAS EMISSIONS: Harvest and Transport	Harvest, transport, and milling emissions included*	-
	Infrastructure construction emissions excluded	Eberle et al. 2007
	Transport emissions of finished products to market were excluded	-
	Harvest productivity	Table 11; FPInovations 2005
	Transport emissions	Table 12; Gingras and Farveau 1996; Klawer 1995
	3.794 kg CO_2e per liter of diesel combusted (stationary) 3.46 kg CO_2e per liter of diesel combusted (mobile; e.g. transport)	Waldron et al. 2006
	Emissions from extraction, transportation, and combustion of fossil fuels*	Table 13; Deluchi 1991; Gomez et al. 2006
Manufacturing Energy and Emissions Factors	Wood product manufacturing emissions*	Table 15; many sources - see table
	Pulp and paper mill emissions*	Table 11 and 15; Francis et al. 2002

Hennigar, Chris; Amos-Binks, Luke; Cameron, Ryan; Gunn, John; MacLean,
David A.; Twery, Mark. 2013. **ForGATE – A Forest Sector Greenhouse Gas
Assessment Tool for Maine: Calibration and Overview.** Gen. Tech. Rep.
NRS-116. Newtown Square, PA: U.S. Department of Agriculture, Forest Service,
Northern Research Station. 54 p.

This report describes the background calibration, inputs, and outputs of ForGATE,
a forest sector greenhouse gas (GHG) accounting tool designed primarily to
communicate information relevant to the evaluation of projected net GHG exchange
in the context of Maine's forests, the Northeast forest sector, and alternative
national or regional carbon (C) accounting guidelines. It also provides forest
managers and policy makers with an easy-to-use tool for examining the relative
merit (C credit revenue vs. project cost) of C offset projects and forest sector life
cycle GHG accounting. GHG accounts include: 1) storage in aboveground and
belowground live biomass and dead organic matter components; 2) storage in forest
products in use and in landfill; 3) forest sector emissions by harvest, transport,
and mills, or avoided emissions (substitution, bioenergy); as well as 4) landfill
methane release and avoided emissions from methane energy capture. Different
forest and forest product pools can be included in result summaries to reflect
different C accounting guidelines (e.g., Climate Action Reserve, Voluntary Carbon
Standard). Results can be compared for baseline and C offset project scenarios.
Where possible, the marginal differences between baseline and project scenario
performance indicators are calculated. All forest-level emission or storage measures
are expressed in tonnes of CO_2 equivalents for comparison purposes. Finally,
economic indicators such as net present value and benefit-cost ratios for C offset
projects can be evaluated using alternative assumptions for the value of stumpage,
C credits, and offset project costs. The user enters their own inventory of stand type
area by treatment regime data for baseline and offset project scenarios and can
quickly adjust many GHG accounting parameters. ForGATE is available without
charge from http://www.nrs.fs.fed.us/tools/forgate/.

KEY WORDS: carbon sequestration, forest management, forest products,
greenhouse gas, life cycle assessment, carbon credits,
decision support, net present value

Printed on recycled paper

Northern Research Station

www.nrs.fs.fed.us